architecture + process

gehry talks

architecture + process

gehry talks

Frank O. Gehry and Associates

Mildred Friedman, editor
with an essay by Michael Sorkin and
commentaries by Frank O. Gehry

 RIZZOLI
NEW YORK

First published in the United States of America in 1999 by
Rizzoli International Publications, Inc.
300 Park Avenue South
New York NY 10010

Library of Congress Cataloging-in-Publication Data
Gehry talks: architecture + process/
        Mildred Friedman, editor; with an essay by
        Michael Sorkin; commentaries by Frank O. Gehry and Associates.
                p.   cm.
        Includes bibliographical references and index
        ISBN 0-8478-2165-X (hc)
        1. Frank O. Gehry and Associates. 2. Architectural practice,
International. 3. Architecture, Postmodern. 4. Architecture
designs and plans.
I. Friedman, Mildred S. II. Sorkin, Michael, 1948–
III. Frank O. Gehry and Associates
NA737. F69 G45 1999
720'.92—dc21   99-23336
                               CIP

Book design: Tracey Shiffman
Assistant designer: Hillary Sunenshine
Photo editing: Tracey Shiffman and Keith Mendenhall
Cover photo: Whit Preston and Tracey Shiffman
Cover tritone scan and film: Gardner Lithograph, Los Angeles

All freehand sketches are by Frank O. Gehry

Printed and bound in Japan

opposite:
design process model of the
Nationale-Nederlanden Building
Prague, Czech Republic, 1992–1996

overleaf:
sketch for the Walt Disney
Concert Hall, Los Angeles, 1987–

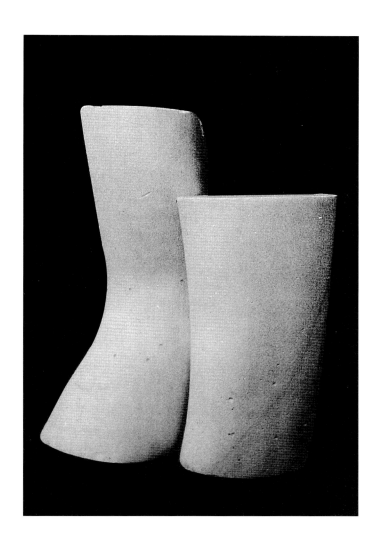

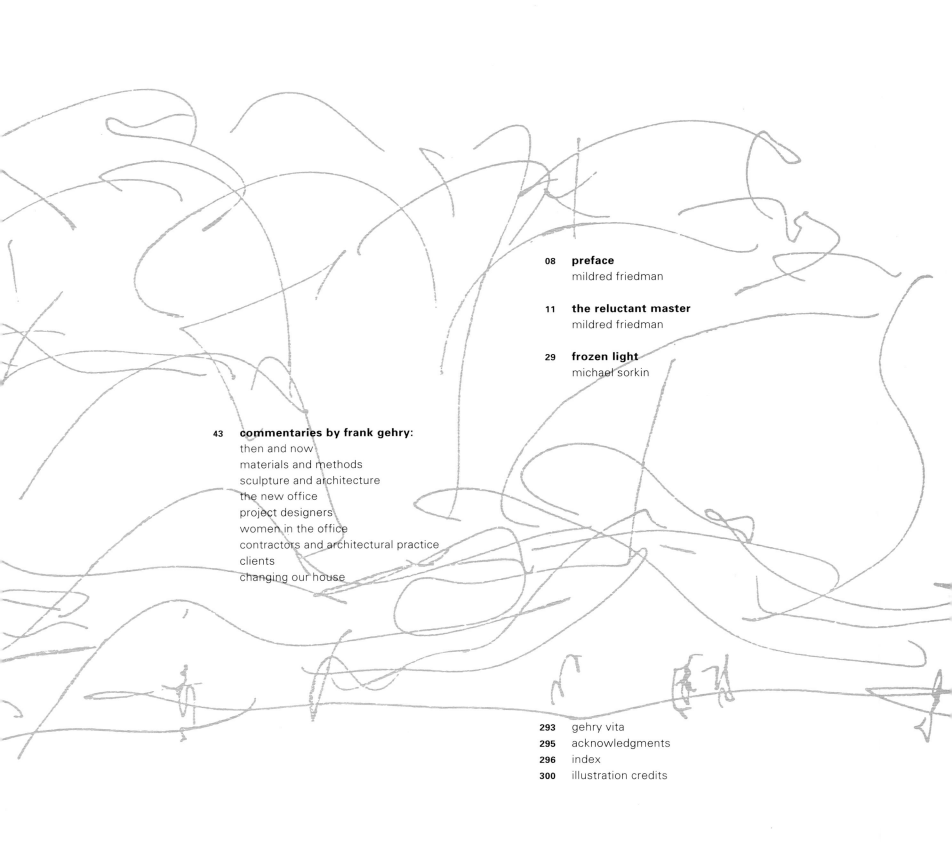

More than any other architect of his generation, Frank Gehry is an innovator whose vision reaches beyond the accepted aesthetic and technical constraints of twentieth-century architecture. His singular formal/philosophical stance developed slowly. In the late 1950s and 1960s—the earliest years of his practice—his work was well planned and handsome, and those who knew it regarded him as a genuine talent. But it wasn't until the 1970s that the box began to break apart, and by the end of that decade he had ventured into absolutely unknown territory with his own "dumb little house"—a small, pink Santa Monica bungalow. It became a laboratory in which it was possible to try anything, and he did. Since then, many barriers to self-expression have come down at his bidding. And in the years since 1989, "smart machines," and the people who operate them, have given him the long-hoped-for freedom to create ever more inventive ways to enclose space.

The means with which Gehry pursues new possibilities and processes have been the focus of my conversations with him over the last several years. From that series of engaging sessions we have extracted a distinctive, revealing body of commentaries by the architect. They form the essential substance of this book. In my introductory essay I examine the significance to his work of various clients, collaborators, and technologies that have greatly affected his practice over the past ten years. Michael Sorkin provides a perceptive view of Gehry's recent work, in which he includes a unique response to the character and quality of the architect's celebrated Guggenheim Museum in Bilbao.

As Gehry's work is about gradual evolution—the development of a project as it takes shape through a long series of physical models—we can only imagine the final forms of a number of works included here that are still in their initial planning phases. Among these is a 1998 commission to produce a study for a proposed Venice Gateway, a passenger terminal and conference center between the airport and Italy's city of light and water. This undertaking promises an opportunity for Gehry to realize the first major work by a non-Italian architect for this most beautiful of all ancient cities, and to once again demonstrate his seemingly unlimited creative energy.

Where will Gehry go from here? I believe that although he denies it (maintaining that he wants to own a winery), he is only truly happy when he is challenged by complex architectural problems. More are certain to come his way.

8

contruction of the Nationale-Nederlanden Building's rooftop sculpture, *Medusa,* made of mesh metal strips

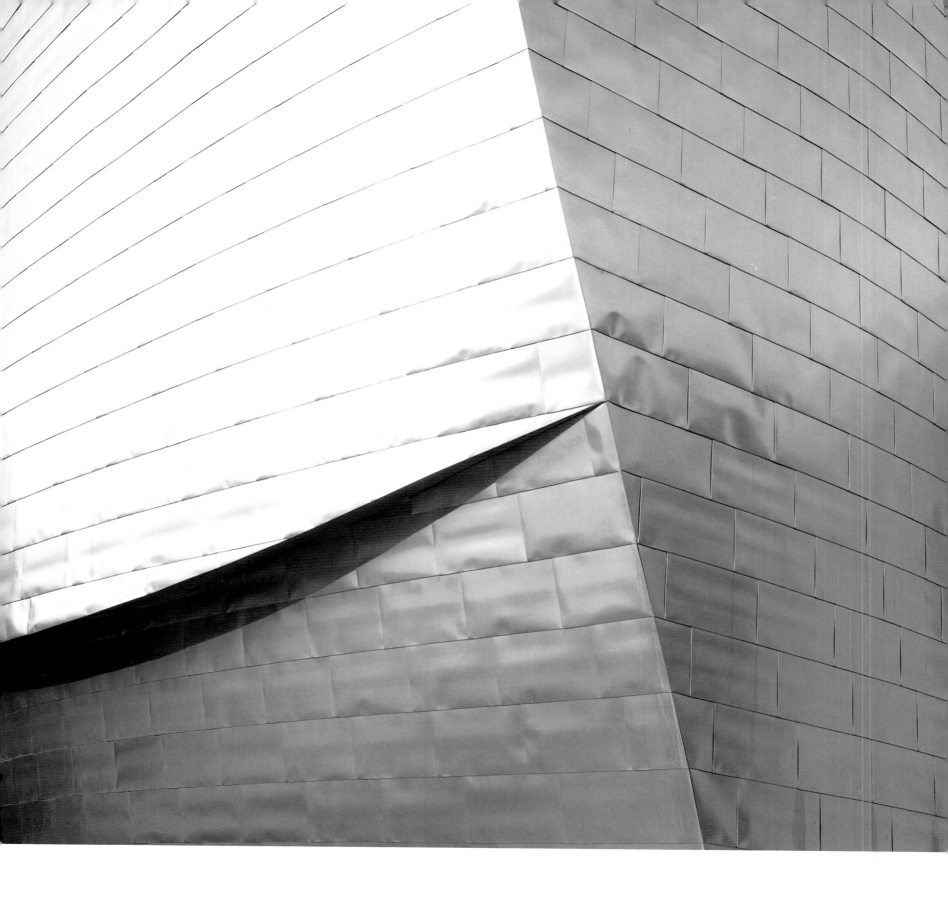

the reluctant master mildred friedman

*To advertise perfection
is beneath Gehry's love of
imperfect humanity.*
—PETER SCHJELDAHL, 1997[1]

Frank Gehry's uncommonly inventive, eccentric architecture—unlike any other—challenges received wisdom. Consequently, his built works elicit diverse responses, both critical and quotidian. Some people are uncomfortable with the formal aspects of the work, and never get beyond them to examine the ways his buildings work; thus, in earlier days, he ruefully remarked that, "Being accepted isn't everything." But with the opening of the Guggenheim Museum in Bilbao he seems to have crossed an invisible line. International awareness and admiration of Gehry's work has subsequently taken on proportions known to very few architects (in Los Angeles, he's a reluctant "celebrity"), and now he spends about half his time traveling to far-flung project sites throughout the United States, Europe, and Asia. He is an inspiring father figure to many young Los Angeles practitioners, and although there is definitely not a FOG "school" as such, many aspiring designers train in his office, and he regularly passes projects along to the courageous hopefuls who venture out on their own.

But success has not spoiled Frank Gehry; rather, it has given him the self-assurance he needed to persevere with his singular experiments with materials and form. He chooses materials both for their formal qualities and their associations. And while his decision to work with plywood, galvanized metal, lead, cardboard, and the much despised, ubiquitous chain-link fencing can be traced in part to the constraints of small budgets, more significant was his desire to demonstrate that chain link, despite its negative associations, can be a positive design element. The Santa Monica Place sign, embedded in veils of blue and white chain link, which covers the south facade of the mall's parking garage, is a daring demonstration of this concept, as is Gehry's notorious 1978 remodeling of his wood-framed Santa Monica house.

The seeds of much that was to come are in that small, pink California bungalow. For example, in the idiosyncratic form of the kitchen window, we see the first instance of implied motion in Gehry's architecture, in this case derived perhaps from cubism. Here too, the exposure of the house's original wood frame (a gesture that would later be mis-termed "deconstruction") is seen against the "in-process" new house layered around the old one. The recent renovation of the

the Gehry House kitchen,
Santa Monica, California, 1978

11

opposite:
detail of titanium cladding,
Guggenheim Museum
Bilbao, Spain, 1997

house—a controlled effort on Gehry's part to create a more comfortable, accommodating environment for his wife and grown children—lacks, by his own admission, the gentle madness of the original effort.[2] Still, the house retains a monumental quality; it is a paean to individuality, perception, and creativity.

Over the years, as his project budgets have grown, Gehry's choice of materials has become more diverse and esoteric, as in Bilbao, where motion is realized in the building's fluttering titanium skin. For the American Center in Paris, Gehry's effort to be contextual was decisive in his choice of the limestone walls, quarried, appropriately, in France. "I love the stone of Paris. It's like the stucco of L.A.,"[3] he maintains. The Center's zinc roof is his homage to the Hôtel de Ville, and the canopy on the park side of the building conjures a melting mansard roof. Cast glass, a material new to Gehry, will be used to define the seating areas in the Condé Nast Cafeteria project in New York City. Kurt Forster asserts that, "At his best, Gehry manages to free his projects from typological constraints, enabling his buildings to assume shapes of unprecedented kind and configuration."[4] In that regard, Gehry explains that "you can't redo old ideas. The only way to gain is to go forward and not look back. You can learn from the past, but you can't continue to be in the past."[5]

All of Frank Gehry's adult years have been spent in Los Angeles (where he moved with his family from Toronto, at the age of sixteen), with only two short breaks: Harvard's Graduate School of Design, and a sojourn in Paris with the French firm of André Remondet. But it is Los Angeles—unique city of slender palms and smog-shrouded freeways—that spawned this rare imagination.

left and center: Dennis Keeley, freeway infrastructure, Los Angeles, 1996 gelatin-silver prints, courtesy the artist

Lewis Baltz, from *The New Industrial Parks near Irvine, California,* 1974 gelatin-silver print, courtesy the artist

12

Gehry's early influences were the great southern California modernists—Raphael Soriano, Richard Neutra, and Harwell Harris. All three were at the top of their form in the 1950s when Gehry was studying at the University of Southern California. But the freewheeling nature of his attitude toward materials and form matured in the 1960s in concert with those of a group of Los Angeles artists, including Edward Moses, Robert Irwin, Billy Al Bengston, Chuck Arnoldi, Ron Davis, Larry Bell, Edward Ruscha, and Kenneth Price. As the beauty of California's extraordinary natural light is an essential element in the work of these artists, it is also a hallmark of Gehry's architecture. But these artists not only respond to southern California's natural environment. In addition, a play on the characteristic "L.A." vernacular is consistently present in their works, as it is in Gehry's. What he refers to as the "urban junkyard" of disparate styles inspired his breakthrough architecture, in which stucco, plywood, chain link, and corrugated metal reflect the context of his city. Beyond the materiality of the Los Angeles cityscape there is the myth and mystery of Hollywood. For although Gehry has never worked in the industry, many of his friends and clients are part of that world, and inevitably, in subtle ways, he responds to its presence, and expresses its influence in the exuberant cinematic movement that often animates his work.

In the 1980s, Gehry's horizons expanded, as did his awareness of artists outside of Los Angeles and his references to diverse environments. In New York, his friendships have evolved into memorable collaborations with Richard Serra, Claes Oldenburg and Coosje van Bruggen. At the same time, his office walls are covered with

Daniel J. Martinez, 4th Street Bridge, Los Angeles, 1998
gelatin-silver print, courtesy the artist

[2] See Gehry's discussion of the remodeling, (p. 57).

[3] Cathleen McGuigan in *Newsweek*, 13 June 1994.

[4] From Kurt W. Forster, "Architectural Choreography," in *Frank O. Gehry: The Complete Works* by Kurt W. Forster and Francesco Dal Co (New York: The Monacelli Press, 1998).

[5] Unless otherwise noted, all quotations from Frank Gehry, staff members of Frank O. Gehry & Associates, and Gehry clients are taken from interviews with the author in 1997 and 1998.

Roland Young
No. 105, Century Freeway,
Los Angeles, 1990
gelatin-silver print,
courtesy the artist

13

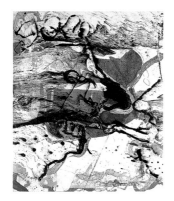

magazine clippings and postcard images of great historic works by such masters as Claus Sluter, Gentile Bellini, and Constantin Brancusi, artists who inspire him and, in subtle ways, influence his architecture. Figuration, which began with Gehry's famously quirky fish fascination, is a growing aspect of his work. It is present in the dancing figures in Prague, the horse's head first found in the Lewis house and later realized in the DG Bank on Berlin's Pariser Platz and, less specifically, in the organic baroquery characteristic of all the recent work.

As Gehry has gradually developed his own increasingly daring sculptural forms, his collaborations with artists have been fewer. However, his enthusiasm for old and new art has not diminished and occasionally he demonstrates his profound understanding of works of art in exhibition installations for the Los Angeles County Museum of Art, Los Angeles's Museum of Contemporary Art, and the Guggenheim museums. Exhibition projects and his design of furniture and lamps provide Gehry with something architecture cannot: instant gratification, quick nourishment—what he has called "fast food"—a diet he enjoys when its substance captures his imagination. Memorable early installations for

Ed Moses
Ranken and ¹/₂, 1992
oil on canvas
60 x 48 inches
courtesy LA Louver

Richard Serra
Torqued Ellipse I, 1996
Cor-ten steel
installation at The Geffen
Contemporary, Museum of
Contemporary Art,
Los Angeles, 1999
Dia Center for the Arts, New York

Edward Ruscha
Hollywood, 1968
silk-sceen print
17 ¹/₂ x 44 inches
courtesy of the artist

the Los Angeles County Museum of Art included *The Avant-Garde in Russia, 1910–1930,* in 1980, and *German Expressionist Sculpture* in 1983.

For the Musée des Arts Décoratifs in Montreal, Gehry created an environment of ingeniously designed movable display cases in 1992. The cases are arrayed in a rather low-ceilinged area, presumably a temporary space in Moshe Safdie's Musée des Beaux-Arts de Montréal, in lieu of the decorative arts museum's hoped-for building of its own. Carefully crafted of plywood and thick plate glass, these remarkable vitrines, in a variety of sizes and surprising shapes, were designed to accommodate the museum's permanent collection, and Gehry has accomplished that charge with amazing verve.

In 1998 Gehry designed the Guggenheim's *Art of the Motorcycle* exhibition, an examination of the evolution of the bikes beloved by Thomas Krens (himself an "easy rider"), director of the Solomon R. Guggenheim Foundation in New York. One hundred of these amazing machines were shown chronologically on Frank Lloyd Wright's astonishingly transformed mirror-finished, stainless-steel-lined ramp. The most engaging elements of the exhibition were in two of the museum's side galleries. Bikes, as though in motion, were arranged on daunting hills whose ribbon-like black and white vinyl surfaces were laid over elegantly configured exposed wood under-structures that careened to challenging heights.

permanent collection installation
in Gehry's plywood and glass vitrines
Musée des Arts Décoratifs de
Montréal, 1992

The Art of the Motorcycle
exhibition installation by
Frank O. Gehry & Associates at the
Solomon R. Guggenheim Museum,
New York, 1998

the office. In 1989 there were about twenty people in the Gehry office. There were two computers—one word processor and one in accounting. At that time Gehry worked with outside executive architects on major projects.[6] That relationship, still standard practice in many firms today, often leads to misunderstandings, errors in construction, and increased costs. In Gehry's case, the most notorious example of the way in which the executive architect system can go wrong is found in the saga of the Walt Disney Concert Hall—a situation that, as they say, will live in infamy. Because Gehry's 1988 design for the Hall was complex and not thoroughly understood by the executive architect, the estimates generated from their work were astronomical and the project came to a grinding halt. Only the underground parking facility was constructed. While additional funds were being raised, radical changes in Gehry's office structure were underway as he realized that in-house technical expertise of a higher order than he had had in the past was essential to his growing practice. He turned to Jim Glymph, who joined the office on the condition that they would no longer split the work with outside executive architects, but would develop the essential in-house technical expertise that would permit them to develop projects from beginning to end. That is what Frank was looking for. And finally, by the summer of 1998, after ten years of Sturm und Drang, the realization of Disney Hall—designed and controlled in-house—was assured.

The first opportunity for Glymph to take charge of the whole process came along with the Barcelona fish for the Vila Olimpica, a hotel/commercial development commissioned for the 1992 summer Olympic Games, and created in collaboration with Bruce Graham of Skidmore Owings & Merrill's Chicago office. A steel sculptural element, 177 feet long and 115 feet high, the fish sits atop a retail court. The client was in a hurry, and the office had less than a year to have the project ready for the games. Glymph explains: "We were asking basic questions: what would the process be if you didn't divide projects up into the compartments that have evolved over the last half of the twentieth century? If you just tried to do what was necessary to get the job done, how would you conceive of carrying out the process?"

After looking at a variety of systems that couldn't do the job, Glymph found software created by Dassault Systèmes for the French aerospace industry. The answer was the Catia program, designed to represent complex three-dimensional objects. Then the Gehry office found a collaborating contractor in Italy, Massimo Colomban's company Permasteelisa, which bought into the program. Together they made the Barcelona fish happen.

opposite:
Gehry's Barcelona fish sculpture, constructed of woven metal strips, commissioned for the Vila Olimpica, 1992

16

[6] Executive architects are responsible for construction documents. Their role places them between the designer and the contractor, and often, to the detriment of the designer, between the designer and the client.

There is a lot of competition for Catia now. "None of that existed when we started," Glymph points out. "Boeing got into Catia *after* we made the Barcelona fish. (I like saying that.)" In the beginning, Dassault gave the architects a great deal of support, but when Boeing ordered a thousand stations, it all disappeared for a while, because with repetitive, mass-produced products, such as cars and planes, they get their money back. With one-of-a-kind buildings, it was a different story. But Bilbao changed everything, and Dassault now sees the potential in the development of new programs for architects. Nevertheless, architects eventually will develop their own software, and the Gehry team is already well on the way to doing just that.

Most schools teach and most architects use visualization or rendering computer programs. But because Jim Glymph wants to use the computer to get buildings built, there were no graphic rendering programs in the Gehry office for a long time. No pretty pictures. He wants a direct link to the craftsmen who are building the buildings. He explains, "It's the old image of the architect as master builder." Control is back where it belongs, he believes, in the hands of the architect from beginning to end. He points to Prague and Bilbao as projects where they've achieved this goal.

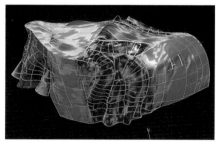
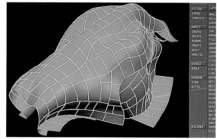
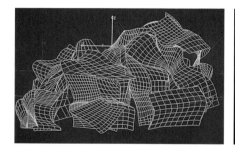
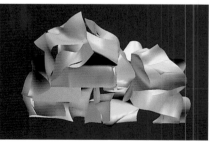

18

**Catia curvature analysis,
Experience Music Project**

**Catia model, conference center,
DG Bank at Pariser Platz**

**Catia cladding study,
Telluride Residence**

**Catia shaded surface study,
Telluride Residence**

Newer projects where this is happening are in the pre-casting of the concrete for the office buildings in Dusseldorf, the free-form metal on the Experience Music Project in Seattle, and the formed glass for Condé Nast in New York. In these projects they see the beginning of a new way of working, now tentatively termed the Architecture-Engineering-Construction Industry.

Most of the momentum in the development of new software is designed to serve the large conglomerates—Fleur, Bechtel, Takanaka—with staffs of thousands and few designers in sight. For small, independent designers to compete, new working methods have to be developed, such as video teleconferencing and applications sharing. Glymph maintains that, "If the big companies get there first, they will set the standards and we'll be back with the old divided process again—what Frank wanted to get away from." So, the Gehry office is attempting to set a model for small offices, and as the programs become more affordable, this could happen. At this point, with the computer, they can work out any bugs that may occur in construction, and they can accurately figure quantities and costs. Those abilities are changing the practice of architecture.

Richard Smith, a high-powered technical whiz who came to the office with the Catia program, describes how an elevation was delineated before the computer. "The architects built a box that had a frosted glass window, and they set up an elevation. They'd shine a light from behind the box, which would cast a shadow on the frosted glass. Then they'd take tracing paper, trace the shadow, and they'd say, 'Well, that's our elevation.' I came in and asked, 'How do you know that the dimensions are right?' And they told me, 'Hey, Michelangelo did this. This is the way it's been done for centuries. Don't buck it.'"

That was then. Now the question is, How does Gehry fit into the new process? His working method hasn't changed because of the computer; however, it has made it easier for his collaborators to achieve many of his most eccentric forms. He still develops his ideas slowly, from sketches through a long series of physical models. "I sit and I watch and I move things. I move a wall, I move a piece of paper, I move something, and I look at it—and it evolves."[7] The difference is in what happens next. A computer device digitizes the model information with absolute accuracy, and the Gehry office builds a virtual building in the computer.

Randy Jefferson, the third member of the Gehry office management triangle, joined the firm in 1992. His job is to make things happen smoothly and properly. His purpose, he explains, is "to create the important balance between excellence in design and excellence in technical development." He helps apply the office's technical systems to specific projects. Bringing all the players together, he solves problems. "If we don't know how to build it," he believes, "it's unlikely that others are going to figure it out." So in looking for people to work with—engineers, contractors, etc.— "we are after people who know how to think and who know how to use the computer as a tool. We're dealing with a very interesting corner of architecture where new thresholds are being defined with each project."

Jefferson believes that one of the fundamental differences between Gehry and many other architects is that "Frank cares more about his clients than all the rest put together. If there were not that caring, you'd just throw up your hands, because it's just a game. It's game-playing and ego. It's not that he doesn't have an ego. And then it gets down to another principle: It doesn't matter how good the architect is; in the

[7] From Charles Gandee, "Spanish Conquest." *Vogue*, October 1997.

end, the building is only as good as the client."

It is apparent that Gehry's most successful projects are the result of a lively interaction between the architect and his clients. If there is no interaction, there are no ideas. And as his process evolves slowly, there is time for relationships to grow, for exchanges to become natural and to the point. But sometimes the architect-client relationship fails and Gehry's interest wanes in the resulting work. For various reasons, Gehry has never visited the completed Iowa Advanced Technology Laboratories at the University of Iowa or the Herman Miller Manufacturing Facility and the Sirmai-Peterson residence, both in California. It is not that these projects are failures—Gehry believes that Sirmai-Peterson may be his best house yet—but he maintains that "making buildings is a personal thing. You create a relationship with people and if that changes, or the people change, the project is not so interesting. The building is a building, but it has lost its soul."

some clients. Jay Chiat is one of Gehry's most loyal clients. He has commissioned several office projects and a vacation house in Telluride, which is still in the hopper. An advertising executive, Chiat met Gehry in the early 1980s when he was looking for a place to locate his company's offices (Chiat/Day) in the Los Angeles area. Having rejected conventional "square" spaces in office buildings as incompatible with the kind of creative work environment he wanted, he decided on a site in Venice, which, incidentally was owned by Frank Gehry and his associate, Greg Walsh. However, before they had progressed very far, toxic waste (coal tar) was discovered on the site. During the years it took to eliminate the harmful materials, Gehry designed a temporary office for the company in a nearby warehouse building on Hampton Drive.

That situation gave him an unexpected opportunity, similar to one he would have later with the Los Angeles Museum of Contemporary Art's Temporary Contemporary space: a huge, high-ceilinged, wood-framed warehouse that permitted free play for off-beat ideas. At Chiat/Day the most memorable element was a larger version of the headless/tailless fish form Gehry had first created for his 1986 Walker Art Center retrospective exhibition. The scale change allowed it to become a 54-foot-long communal room in which Gehry's friend, the psychiatrist Milton Wexler, often held conferences. Later, Dr. Wexler wrote:

> The conference center Frank created for the Chiat/Day Temporary office interior was nothing but a whale. Inside this lovely curved space, a huge conference table allowed for all kinds of informal meetings. The sound was perfect. In some strange way, one could almost feel that this was a marvelous environment in which to give birth to great ideas. In the belly of a whale, one felt enclosed, nurtured, protected, prompted to play, to experiment, to break out of the commonplace.

Gehry also successfully designed Chiat/Day's Toronto office interior and made an unrealized attempt in New York. When Chiat/Day's Venice Headquarters building was in process in 1989, Claes Oldenburg and Coosje van Bruggen designed the incredible binocular conference rooms that are the central element in the building's tripartite facade. The binoculars, together with Gehry's "boat" form on one side and copper-clad "trees" on the other, have created an unforgettable Main Street landmark.

During the years of his long friendship with Chiat, Gehry has been the recipient of an incredible number of prestigious awards: The Pritzker Prize, the Wolf Foundation Prize, the Praemium Imperiale, the Dorothy and Lillian Gish Award, and the National Medal of the Arts, along with innumerable other significant honors. Thus, Chiat recently quipped, "because Frank is accepting all these awards, he's going to peak too soon. By the time he's ninety, he will have had it. If they call him up and want to give him an award, he should say, 'No, I'm sorry, I can't do February. If you'll do this in April....'" In a more serious vein, Chiat continued, "I think he has incredible instincts that he translates into impulsive gestures, and because his instincts are so good and his intuition is so honed, the results are perfect." He relates, for example, that Gehry conceived the Chiat/Day Main Street headquarters building in his very first sketch for it on a restaurant tablecloth in Santa Monica. "When we left the restaurant someone asked, 'Do you have the tablecloth?' I said no, we've got to go back and get it. I retrieved the tablecloth, and it is the building." (Although finding the fin-

interiors of the Chiat/Day
Temporary Offices,
Venice, California, 1986–1988

opposite:
design process model for
Jay Chiat's house,
Telluride, Colorado, 1998

ished building, "getting it right," in this very early sketch seems to contradict the long evolutionary process that Gehry works through on every project—in fact, both phenomena are true.)

In the 1960s, Penny and Mike Winton moved into an elegant suburban house near Minneapolis that had been designed in 1952 by Philip Johnson, in his early Miesian manner. As their five children began to marry and have their own families in the early 1980s, the Wintons realized that they didn't have enough room for family visits in the main house, and they asked Johnson to design a guest house. At the time he begged off, maintaining he was too busy, but he agreed to call them with suggestions. Nine months went by with no call. Then on 16 May 1982 the Wintons opened the *New York Times Magazine* to an article by Joseph Morgenstern, and they agreed, "This is it!" The article was all they knew about Frank Gehry.

Mike Winton remembers that soon after their Sunday epiphany, they visited the early houses Gehry had designed in Venice and the Aerospace Museum addition in Los Angeles's Exposition Park, which had just been finished. "But Loyola Law School was the one that really blew us away—Penny and I were hooked." They were drawn to the work for several reasons. There was "such self-confidence, he didn't have to

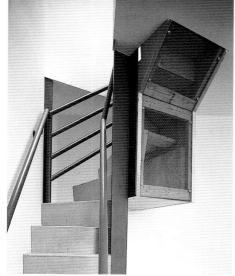

borrow, and there was so much wit." They didn't give Gehry a rigid program. Primarily, they wanted the house to be amusing and welcoming to children, so that they would want to keep coming to visit grandma and grandpa. During the process, Mike repeatedly told Gehry they couldn't afford it. Almost four years went by, and Mike kept saying, "Frank, I have to wait until my ship comes in." Then one day Gehry came in, looked at Mike and said, "Mike, your friends tell me your ship is in."

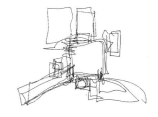

Penny remembers, "We had a budget of, I think, $450,000, something like that. And at that time, we were his first 'luxury' client. When we got to the bathrooms, he wanted to do them in marble or stone, and I kept saying, 'Uh...let's have some plywood.' And on the staircase, when he came through during construction and saw the inner workings of the staircase up to the little room, I said, I really love seeing that; I don't want to shut it off behind wallboard, and he said, 'Don't do this to me. I'm trying to live down my reputation as a junk architect.'"

That unlikely beginning resulted in one of Gehry's most significant projects. Seen across the gently sloping site from the vantage of the Johnson house, the windowless west facades of the Winton guest house appear as a collection of singular forms clad in limestone, brick, sheet metal, and Finnish plywood. The iconic pinwheel plan and its four interconnected structures constitute an expressive work that prefigures the sculptural character of many designs to follow.

Michael Eisner met Gehry not as Disney's CEO, but as a hockey enthusiast. Both families play and they found each other at a hockey rink. Eisner was aware of Gehry's work in the chain-link era, and had admired his progress for many years. Their first project together was the Entertainment Center for Euro-Disney (now called Disneyland Paris), a complex project that left Gehry less than satisfied. They later went on to the ice rink and Disneyland Headquarters, both in Anaheim, California.

Eisner admires Gehry's work because he finds it "aggressive, challenging, and risky." The ice rink is Eisner's favorite Gehry building. Its voluptuous biomorphic exterior, which Eisner describes as a woman lying on her back, is sheathed in corrugated anodized aluminum. The interior practice rink for Anaheim's Mighty Ducks is lined with laminated wood beams—warm and welcoming— "reflecting Gehry's love of hockey." Eisner believes that "it's simple and great."[8]

Available Light, choreography by
Lucinda Childs, set by Frank Gehry,
was performed at the opening of
the Temporary Contemporary,
Museum of Contemporary Art,
Los Angeles, 1983

opposite:
Winton Guest House, interior stair
and view of south elevation (right),
Wayzata, Minnesota, 1987

sketch for the pinwheel plan,
Winton Guest House, 1985

Disney Ice, Anaheim, California,
1993–1996

One of Gehry's most supportive Los Angeles clients is Richard Koshalek, the former director of the Museum of Contemporary Art and the Temporary Contemporary
(now The Geffen Contemporary), L.A.'s guerrilla museum, in the heart of Little
Tokyo. In 1983, Koshalek invited the choreographer Lucinda Childs to create an inau-
gural dance work for the TC, and he commissioned Gehry to design the set and com-
poser John Adams, the music. Titled *Available Light,* this work was performed on a
double platform seen from three sides, surrounded by a scrim of chain link.[9] It was
an astonishing success, and soon after, Gehry was commissioned to renovate the
warehouse. The tiny budget for the remodeling was raised through the sale of prints
donated by eight artists. Designated "temporary," while the museum by Arata
Isozaki was under construction, this simple, industrial structure continues to house
many of MOCA's most important exhibitions, and its entry and street facade are currently being revised in order to better accommodate future exhibition and performing
arts projects. Koshalek believes that the building's most successful quality is its infor-
mality, its accessibility; it is as close as a museum can come to the environment of an
artist's studio. Thus, the widely accepted ideal of the clean white neutral space is one
that Gehry has proven inadequate in all of his subsequent museum projects.

Koshalek later chaired the committee that selected Gehry as the architect for the
Walt Disney Concert Hall. When the project ran into fiscal difficulties, MOCA mounted

[8] See Gehry's assessments of
Euro-Disney (p.116) and the ice
rink (p. 218), which are somewhat
at odds with those of Eisner.

[9] See Mildred Friedman, "Fast
Food," in *The Architecture of
Frank Gehry* (Minneapolis, New
York: Walker Art Center/Rizzoli,
1986), 101-104.

an exhibition of drawings and models for the Hall to demonstrate the significant role it could play in the cultural life of the city and the downtown neighborhood in which the museum and the new Hall are primary players.

Gehry's most celebrated museum commission to date is the Guggenheim Museum Bilbao in Spain's northern-most Basque city. And consequently, Thomas Krens is currently Gehry's most widely known client. The project began in 1991 when Krens invited Gehry to visit an old warehouse building the Basques were proposing for the museum. Neither believed the building would work as the site for a museum, and they agreed that a central city location along the Nervión River would be ideal. Three firms were then invited to participate in a competition for the design of the building: Coop-Himmelblau, Arata Isozaki, and Frank O. Gehry & Associates. The jury included Basque government officials, a Spanish museum director, and a curator; Heinrich Klotz, director of the German Architecture Museum in Frankfurt, was referee.

atrium of the Guggenheim Museum Bilbao, Spain, 1997

opposite:
view of the Guggenheim Museum Bilbao seen from across the Nervión River, 1997

The selection of Gehry was the beginning of a six-year collaboration between Gehry and perhaps his most hands-on client. Krens asserts that "Great architecture is not just a question of pure genius per se; it's a function of opportunity." The program was simple: 300,000 square feet, of which 150,000 would be exhibition space. "The building had to embrace an existing bridge over the river, and be equally hospitable to a 200-ton Richard Serra sculpture and a Picasso drawing." Krens wanted an atrium plan. He believes that Wright's New York Guggenheim works well and he wanted a building in which the atrium would always provide a point of orientation, and not be simply an entrance hall. Krens suggested that "the dominant model for the atrium should be a cathedral such as Chartres." Gehry began with three other metaphors: Fritz Lang's film *Metropolis*, Brancusi's Paris studio, and a rock quarry in Indiana. He eventually discarded the image of the rock quarry. Krens believes that Gehry has "a greater faith in process than any other architect. The thing about Bilbao is the surprise of it." Entering the lobby is truly an exhilarating experience: "Walking into [its] main atrium is like tossing your cap in the air."[10] After the atrium and the 450-foot-long gallery, the last things one expects to see are what Gehry calls the "stodgy" galleries. But these classical spaces are perfectly suited to works from the Guggenheim's early-twentieth-century collection, which will often be shown there. Herbert Muschamp, writing about the museum for the *New York Times Magazine*, concludes: "Critics don't have to say 'yes, but'; it's all right to say something's really good. You don't have to qualify it."

Gehry's remarkable building, together with the long overlooked city's first subway system, designed by the English architect Norman Foster, Santiago Calatrava's pedestrian bridge and planned airport, and the music hall by Federico Soriano and Dolores Palacios, plus several other proposed projects, promise a brighter future for this revitalized Basque city. If the Bilbao experience, in all of its manifestations, proves a success, it could make believers of the most skeptical among us. In its example, we sense the possibility that significant architecture and brilliant planning can change both the face and the spirit of the world's oft-neglected cities.

24

[10] J. Carter Brown, in a letter to Ada Louise Huxtable, 9 March 1998.

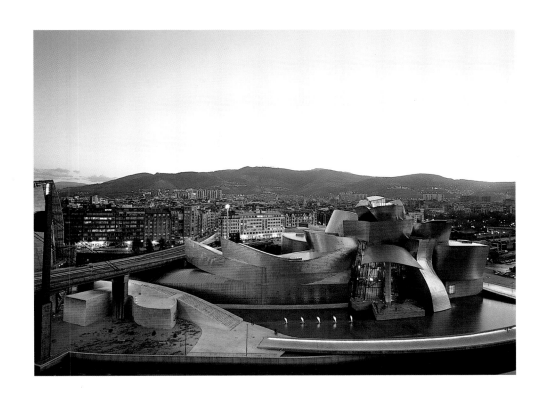

The 1986 Walker Art Center exhibition, *The Architecture of Frank Gehry*, was a
celebration of twenty-five years of work by this American original, then not widely
known outside the inner circles of new architecture. That exhibition experience (four
years in the making) was my trial-by-fire introduction to Gehry's singular working
method. For the Walker exhibition he created five full-scale elements using lead, copper, cardboard, plywood, and Finnish plywood. These structures demonstrated various ways he uses materials and, at the same time, housed drawings, photographs,
and models of his realized projects. Thus, while seeing the exhibition, the viewer was
also experiencing a full-size Gehry space. His ability to inform, by making it possible
for the observer to interact with the exhibition, provided a vital link to the meaning
inherent in the works on view. To demonstrate how architecture happens—how an
idea goes from Gehry's initial sketch to a realized project—was attempted there and
is our purpose here, where we take up his story post 1986.

frozen light michael sorkin

In front of Frank Gehry's Guggenheim Museum in Bilbao stands an enormous Jeff Koons topiary puppy. Supported by a complex but unseen armature and enabled by a fiendish system for watering and fertilizing, the floral dog dominates the museum's foreground. I wanted to hate that puppy but found myself charmed...sort of: once the irony was scraped off, beneath lay treacle. Thus laid bare, no longer an appropriation of kitsch, I was able to see the huge dog as pure kitsch—charming, goofy.

Architects I know who had the pleasure of visiting the Guggenheim while it was under construction raved about the beauties of its intricate armature, the rising, cross-braced snakes of steel. Gehry often talks about inspiration drawn from construction sites, buildings that are at their best half done. Part of this is just the modernist aesthetic with its tooth for the forms of engineering and construction. But it also comes from a view that the unfinished version has a special innocence, clarity, authenticity, and authority. Like the childhood of the sketch, the worry is that elaboration and growth inevitably equal loss.

It is one of the many successes of the Guggenheim that it has not simply survived its transformation but that in maturity it has only added density while retaining the vigor, kinks, and visual charm of its skeleton. In the kinetic atrium and in the picturesque tower framed beyond the preexisting bridge—the skeletal armature is both revealed and employed, and the exuberance and complexity of the work-in-progress is retained.

on the entry plaza the topiary puppy, by the artist Jeff Koons, welcomes visitors to the Guggenheim Museum Bilbao

opposite:
atrium of the Guggenheim Museum Bilbao, under construction, 1997

For the foregrounded Koons, though, the armature remains invisible, the dog beneath the skin. Illusionistic, it depends on this invisibility, the backgrounding of its means of support. The dependence of the fuzzy pup on its concealed skeleton is ironical. The Guggenheim—equally histrionic—engages the same problematic as the pup: the elaborate unseen structure required to support the complex family of curved forms. But there's no irony. And this is something that can be said about Gehry's work from the beginning: nothing is concealed, no jokes are made, no self-consciousness is exhibited, no meta-meanings are inscribed.

The Koons puppy is a cartoon. Cartooning idealizes a subject by drawing out some essence. Cartooning is an intermediary state, a subjects become condensed and

malleable. The cartoon prepares a subject for irony, kitsch, or critique. In the case of the Koons, the essentialized pup, stripped of detail and inflated to enormity, opens up a kind of metakitsch, a gigantic hyperbanality. It's this disproportion that gives the work its meaning.

Gehry also makes cartoons, forms full of pared depiction. The mimetic reading is both irresistible, totally legit, and unavoidable. This engages both the obvious sources (all those fish) and a certain incitement to ferret out the metaphor. I've read, among others, a description in which Disney Hall is compared to a flower. It never struck me thus: I am reminded rather of those dancing hippopotami in Disney's *Fantasia*, improbably light of foot. And the building is ineffable in similar wise. Curvy, twisted renditions of shapes that approach familiar platonic forms but that—like cartoon houses—bulge with the energy of (incipient) animation. The building is both beautiful and incredibly apt to its patron.

The invention of the movies was transformative for architecture, paralleling and informing the invention of the idea of space. A medium that allows the continuous depiction of space, the movies goaded architecture into a new sense of flow, creating an idea of the palpability—the physics—of the space. Space was no longer just a byproduct of the order of events. Animated, the rush of space could be expected to have an effect on the material conditions through which it passed. Film was able, for the first time, to capture the blur of speed much the way we—slow to process our own environment—perceive it. Interest in such distortion through attenuation has

view from the north of the Guggenheim Museum Bilbao, under construction, 1997

something of a history, originating in our ability to cross the landscape at increasing speeds—the view from the train or the car. (Remember all those stretched buildings in the sixties "responding" to the view from the road!)

The film conceit is useful to architecture both for its ability to capture the effects of space and for its store of techniques. I'm thinking of the basic technology of film-making, the decomposition of a continuous kinetic activity into a series of static frames, the stills that undergird the motion. This is an uncanny metaphor for architecture, for something that is constructed via a sequence of precisely measured stabilities to produce something that finds its ultimate legibility in motion. Nothing more clearly encapsulates architecture's relationship to the the idea of motion than the photographs of Eadweard Muybridge. Here the idea is not to create motion but to stop it, to decompose and deconstruct it, to add precisely the necessary stasis to open motion to analysis and, ultimately, to reconstitution.

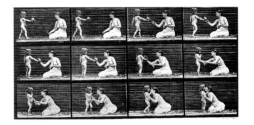

Eadweard Muybridge
Woman and Child, **c. 1877.**
(plate 465 of the Pennsylvania Plates)
Victoria & Albert Museum, London,
Great Britain

Cliffhanger
Chuck Jones
© 1980, Warner Bros.

Which brings us back to cartooning. An animated cartoon is a kind of *gesamtkunstwerk* that, like its cathedral forebears, requires the precisely coordinated assembly of a huge number of individually produced, static elements in order to construct a singularity. A single cartoon cel, then, somehow contains the implication of its successors, the idea that motion, being physical, can be created from its particles. The most revealing and intimate moment in animated cartoons is that familiar image of Wile E. Coyote who, having just barreled over a cliff, takes a few moments to discover that he is running through thin air, looks down, and only then plummets to earth.

The hapless Coyote suggests the idea that physics is also psychical, that there is a moment of ambiguous intersection between gravity and the unconscious, which is true as well for architecture. In Gehry's practice, much weight is put on the sketch, on the spontaneity of impulse and on an essence of ineffable character to which all obeisance must be paid. For Gehry (like Disney), the next step is an inversion. The sketch, which defies conventional geometrical organization, must be translated into a system of precise coordinates and known structural properties, all of which depend on an undergirding Euclideanism. The forms are derived after the fact.

This act suggests a constant tension—constant relationship—between a system of familiar Platonic solids and a set of spontaneous forms that riff but do not ape this set of familiars, much as Mickey resembles a mouse but looks like no mouse we've ever seen. The fantasy is thus inversely symmetrical with the sketch that distorts the unfolding reality it both exaggerates and simplifies. The Disney project is also a distortion, a cartoon that inflates the unseen ideal form: those shapes in Disney Hall are both dancing flowers or hippos but also dancing not-cubes and not-rectangles, distorted away from the familiar but not so far as to cease affinity.

31

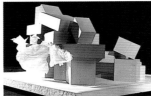

In an interesting insight, Zaha Hadid recently described her early motivation to paint as somehow anticipating the availability of Form-Z, the current Mac-based solid modeling program of choice. The observation is canny in begging the question of animation. If the current architectural avant-garde—indubitably sourced in Gehry's work—has a shared obsession, it's with the motility of architecture. The conceit, not of frozen music but of frozen motion, surely informs a myriad of fantasies of tipping facades and rotating masses, a simulation of instability that has been the hallmark of so much recent work.

Much has been made about the transformation of Gehry's practice to a computer-dominated one. Both too much and too little is implied. Too much because the computer is not used as a generative device but as an instrument of translation: thanks to the computer we can, within the limits of materials and gravity, now build any shape. But the computer also provides another liberation. Secure in the knowledge that anything can be produced, drawing—sketching—is itself emboldened, offering a license that gives the sketch validity not simply as a source but as the final technical authority. The computer enables the representation and manipulation of that which cannot otherwise be drawn.

The current trend in supercomputers is to the massively parallel. Largely out of favor are the incredibly powerful single processors of older machines and in their place hundreds of microprocessors linked together do the job. Tasks are not performed sequentially but divided and their components are solved separately and simultaneously. In many ways, this approach is similar to that of the traditional, pre-computer, handicraft animation studio. To produce the images necessary to inhabit

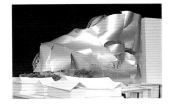

a project's gradual evolution, from
basic wood blocks to indications
of materials and sculptural form,
is demonstrated in this exemplary
series of design process models
for the unrealized Samsung
Museum of Modern Art, in Seoul,
Korea, 1995.

the hundreds of thousands of film frames in a full-blown animated movie, cadres of artists labor for months or years to break down the sequence of animation in the freeze-frame of individual cels and then draw and paint them one by one.

Gehry's use of the computer enables the same process to take place, only backwards. Although the entire object is crunched at once, what is produced is a single model of an extremely complex form, which only the intelligence of the computer can be said to comprehend in its all-at-once. To the observer, the central model can only be constructed by observing the building through a self-propelled animation of every aspect of it, decomposing it into infinite "frozen" views.

For those actually designing the building in its detailed particulars and for those constructing it, the all-at-once is decomposed into a conventional series of working drawings. Although this is likely to change before too long, buildings are still constructed from paper plans, from individual drawings of each and every part to be assembled. However, there is a portion of the process in which the intermediary of a drawing can be obviated, particularly in a case like the mechanical cutting of the doubly curved stone skin at Bilbao, where there was direct communication between the design computer and the machines that milled the stone to shape. There's an interesting gap between the extreme fragility of the sketch and the intense particularity of the construction documents, all of which is negotiated within the computer, that begs interesting questions about the ultimate availability of architectural "expert systems." If one thinks of the computer as no more than a sophisticated pencil, there's no issue. If it has the potential to be more....

It is in this sense that Bilbao might also be described as an intermediary triumph and a harbinger of both greater freedom and license for the computer as architectural generator. Many have described the building as the first of the twenty-first century, although I prefer to think of it as the apotheosis of our own. For Gehry, the computer is a tool, not a partner—an instrument for catching the curve, not for inventing it. His design process also includes repetitive physical modeling in which the computer (in concert with laser measuring devices) becomes a notational partner. Gehry's work, full of genius, does not beg any fundamental questions for art. It is simply beautiful in the old-fashioned way and there is no doubt as to who the artist is.

The technology used in Gehry's office—the Dassault system—is, in fact, a machine for realizing curves, and this obsession with a "naturalistic" curvilinearity is also the culmination of an inquiry that dates back at least to Horta, Sullivan, and Gaudí; is carried on by Aalto (with whom Gehry claims special affinity); and rationalized by Bucky and the plastic Corbusier. For all of these, the mimetic drive is to recruit nature as both collaborator and source. Gehry advances the argument both by his cartooning tactics—rounding off, bloating of forms to create an image of friendliness—and by his pursuit of the limpidity of the "natural," freely drawn curve, with its legato elegance and its suggestion that nature is simply another perceptual system producing its own private styles of distortion.

Louis Kahn asked the brick what it wanted to be and the brick confided that it was an arch. This sense of volition is the gift of functionalism to materials. Frank Gehry's creative breakthrough has long been associated with his craftsman (in the Sears, Roebuck sense) phase. After long association with artists, Gehry turned from the depersonalized architecture of the corporate world, with its abstract, immaterial air, to an architecture with which he was in direct emotional contact, the sort of building

34

you almost imagine yourself able to hand-build, certainly to fully understand. For Gehry, this was an autodidactic architecture, an architecture of renewal. The funky work put an end to a functionalist lineage by refiguring the authority of materials, by offering alternative answers to the question of the inner desires of a two by four.

This was also the moment in which the Gehry persona, the bleeding-hearted Canadian nebbish, also began to be thoroughly mythologized, a phenomenon in which the dissembling Gehry has always artfully collaborated. Indeed, in the Woody Allen culture of wearing one's neurosis on one's sleeve, this was architecture's privilege: to reveal itself, to spill its guts. Like his contemporaries Peter Eisenman (who famously used to claim to have, in the manner of Pascal's wager, both a Jungian and a Freudian shrink) or John Hejduk, the element of autobiography was returned to architecture. That Gehry's breakthrough project was a transformation of his own house is surely significant.

Most accounts of Gehry's turn to the chain-link and corrugated palette devolve on the cheap and ordinary nature of the materials. But I would suggest that the roots of the style derive not from tight-fistedness, but control. Control, to begin, is a question of knowledge, and these works were in a medium the newly independent practitioner could most knowledgeably and efficiently undertake. The turn to the computer as a shape-maker is also a moment of conflation between liberation and control. Gehry's use of materials, in whatever register, is never eccentric. Sheet titanium, as desirous as a brick, wants to be a skin, needs to be laid on the eccentric curves in plates.

So much of art nowadays is forged in the techniques of observation, displaced onto the register of criticism. To this the computer offers an interesting parallel. Like the dislocation of technique in a criticism-driven art, the computer engenders a subtle shift in the process of creation. The conceptual character of a building's prior imaginative existence—given the truly amazing modeling possibilities of computers—means that it can be observed, for the first time, in a simulacrum of the continuities of reality. The computer becomes a means of cinematizing architecture without building and may (though this is a question for another time) harbinger its eventual annihilation.

Gehry's celebrated aedicular strategy, the collage of one-room buildings to create house ensembles, also embodies a form of control. Here, the idea is to produce a transcendental diagram. A conventional tactic for getting into an architectural program is to produce a bubble diagram in which, like those Muybridge photos, a totality is reduced to a series of manageable components. The Taylorized style of mainstream modernism saw this decomposition as a physical convenience, a means of organizing circulation, hierarchy, and dimension. For Gehry, the dispersal has a more physical aura, a means not of producing hierarchy but autonomy, the instrument of what might be called architectural citizenship.

The fragmentation of Gehry's buildings takes quite a bit of interpretive heat. These building colonies have been described as either psychical or social comments on the fragmentations of modern culture (although critics have also taken the tack that what's embodied is more an idea of the singularity of the individual). Either way, the burden of representation that this tactic of subdivision bears is clearly hermeneutic and not intentional. The fragmentation clarifies by exposing its programmatic parts and is, in this sense, a very modernist gambit. However, where traditional modernists color-coded pipes and ducts or argued for literal transparency, Gehry structures his

work on a different idea of visibility. The sense of boundedness this sometimes inspires (Mike Davis has chastized Gehry's urban work as overly defensive) does not, I think, stem from a sense of hostility to the exterior world but a devotion to the individuality of the architectural object.

While the formal lineage for Gehry's fragmenting strategy surely remembers the forms of villages and small towns—whether the rooftop collection of the Wosk penthouse, the pavilionated Simon House, the Winton Guest House, the Loyola Campus, or the truly amazing and (alas) unbuilt Lewis House—there's another aspect of consequence: tinyness, a conflation of difference and diminutiveness. The history of the little building is an unwritten chapter in the development of architecture but an important one. Certainly, some of the current interest in the question stems from the revival of theory of the past twenty years, in revisiting the idea of the "primitive hut," the putative origin point of architecture. There's something biological about all this: the idea of growth via cellular division. Gehry's projects, as they become increasingly sophisticated, seem progressively to embrace this metaphor.

This having been said, I prefer to see Gehry's aedicular tendency as more of an auto-analytical organ, a means by which he has reinvented his architecture. It's instructive to look through his artistic prehistory, his eight years before the mast at Hideo Sasaki, Pereira & Luckman, Victor Gruen Associates, and André Remondet. Search as one does for hints of things to come, there's little to recommend itself as the harbinger of genius. Acceptable corporate design, always decent, never especially innovative, is the order of those days. The only hint of the future lies in Gehry's long experience with the shopping mall. The paradigmatic mall is binucleated like the family, mama and papa anchors holding up opposite ends of an enclosed family room around which cluster the lesser shops, the children of the arrangement. This mall parti informs many of Gehry's works, from his first big independent project—the actual mall in Santa Monica—through the Loyola Campus, and culminating, after a long voyage, with Bilbao, its specialty spaces deployed around a central "atrium" that organizes the functions that surround it.

The autonomous courtyard is a spectacularly useful architectural device because it can effectively cut loose the surrounding elements to develop their own autonomy. The courtyard, in its voidedness, offers a take-up space, a distributor that cedes the orbiting elements enough slack to develop in an informal system, expanding unconstrained by a hemming figural space that demands that their own geometries be subservient. Strange and eccentric shapes can nose into a flexible central figure that permits them the room to retain their own eccentric integrity.

Gehry speaks frequently of his friendship with and admiration of artists. This influence is literal—an indebtedness for representational courage to Oldenburg, an affinity for curvature to Serra—but what's probably most important is the influence of anxiety. It was art (and Los Angeles) that saved Gehry from the seemingly inescapable consequences of universalism. It may also be from this cadre that Gehry acquired the comforting (and historic) notion that politics can inhere in avant-gardism.

Gehry went to school at the height of the influence of modernism (including time served in the planning program at that Kremlin of modernist-think, Harvard's Graduate

36

School of Design), when certain truths were held to be self-evident. The first of these was the need for generic solutions to architectural problems, for systems rather than objects. And the second was a version of minimalism—functionalism—that singular mix of liberalism and Taylorism with its creepy fantasy of mass subjectivity.

Somewhere inside, Frank was bridling at this. Conscience-full product of a Jewish-Canadian, liberal environment, he wanted to help. But inside, the fish of creativity was wiggling to be free. And here the metaphor may be important. Looking back at that Proustian carp alive in the tub, one reads not just animation but imprisonment, circumscribed desire: fish gotta swim, after all, and in the tub they don't get far. And what object can be said to be less vested with its own desires than the carp become part of that grey lump of gefilte fish (however tasty, not what the fish wants to be). Like a Chinese painting of a fish in which a stroke suffices to animate the shape, Gehry reanimates. He sees the orthodox formal vocabulary of most architecture as lifeless and gets to work, not with the production of an alternative system, an accidental incursion from left field produced not by surrealistic trickery nor a single imaginative leap, but with the breath of new life injected into old forms.

The revision starts slowly at the Davis House, in which the box undergoes a mild, sight-line-generated skewing to produce (along with the skewed wing of Asplund's Snellman House) one of the most seminal twists in the history of architecture. With his own house, Gehry extends his palette of distortions to strategies of decomposition and second skin. Here, the box is not simply distorted geometrically, it's stripped bare. Gehry dances down the line of essence, inquiring how much can be removed and reconfigured before the house disappears. The crummy material palette is, to be sure, a part of this, but there's nothing in the materials Gehry introduces that really stands outside the standard-issue materiality of stick-built homes with their two-by-four construction, chain-link back fences, and asphalted drives—a large part of the point. The box has been broken and this new energy parallels Gehry's own escape from the box of corporate practice to a circumstance in which his newly confident and increasingly articulate desires are able to directly imprint his work, to make something new from the old familiars.

Ron Davis Studio/Residence, Malibu, California, 1972

opposite:
site model of the Loyola Law School campus, Los Angeles, 1981

Having demystified the box via distortion and dematerialization, Gehry is ready to move on to ensemble, to the ways in which uses, not simply forms, go together. The city is the ultimate architectural ensemble and Gehry's urbanism is, at the end of the day, fundamentally respectful of the accumulated conventions of the historic. While the forms may be wild, the strategies of situation are both calm and precise. Bilbao, for example, is brilliant not just in its siting but in the way in which it resolves the primary issue of the Bilbao riverfront, the dramatic sectional drop from the main grade of the town to the river bank. Disney Hall, for all its crazed neo-baroquisms, produces an acropolis in friendly collaboration with its dreary predecessors on Bunker Hill. Santa Monica Place skillfully separates automotive and pedestrian access, a mall that both contains its own anchors and anchors Santa Monica's 3rd Street pedestrian shopping street, which existed only as an idea at the time of the mall's building.

The bringing together of pieces in peaceable assembly is the most urgent creative agenda of Gehry's breakout. Although his architecture is relentlessly alleged to incorporate the genius loci of Los Angeles as one of its most fundamental inspirations, the reading is too often distorted by an identification of the city with tackiness and ephemerality—the shake, rattle, and roll of quakes and slides—and with a general celebration of the city's transient veneer. Slighted in this interpretation are certain

sounder elements, especially a history of local place-making. The film studio complexes, endearing shopping centers like the Farmers Market, bungalow courts, and especially the small pedestrian cul-de-sacs, such as the Crossroads of the World, are clear prototypes for the likes of Edgemar, one of Gehry's most successful ensembles.

As with any village, the crucial questions are about the limits of inclusion in community, the tolerable degrees of difference, and the nature of the public or shared spaces. For Gehry, difference is embodied in shape and material, secondarily in use. Elements express their individuality by standing free, an attitude that both de-inscribes them and that, in offering the possibility of a comprehensive, cubistic view of the element, makes the individual piece more comprehensible as such, vesting it with a kind of citizenship via the autonomy of (perceptual) wholeness.

Naturally, there's a problem with treating forms as citizens inasmuch as formalism always risks superseding the desires of users. But—with our most artistic architect—the user's desire is necessarily to inhabit Gehry's own sense of expression, largely mooting the point, except at its periphery where collective spaces are defined, in their edges, as the residue of individual assembly. And here is the innovation. Although Gehry's collective spaces have carefully nuanced scale and detail, they are seldom recoverable as figures. This is genius, this noumenous creation of a public realm that is drawn out of the private, described in detail only by the individual spaces that define it.

The Guggenheim Bilbao is the Weisman Museum rotated through 180 degrees. One side of the arc is occupied with the convulsive geometry of the stainless-steel facade, the other with rectangular boxes of masonry. Bilbao gives a "functional" logic to this geometrical opposition by creating two different kinds of spaces: geometrical, stone-clad, for "historic" modern art, and free-form, titanium-swaddled for contemporary work. Although there's nothing philosophically necessary in this distinction, it works very well, if only in the sense that all the work in the museum is beautifully housed. The only dysfunctional space is the largest, the huge loft room on the ground floor. Here, the issue is not architectural but the curatorial insistence of trying to display puny-seeming two-dimensional works on its 450-foot-long walls, which inevitably leaves the art diminished.

Frank Gehry's work has remarkable command of direction, something—as opposed to orientation—intrinsic and internal. This begins with an acute sense of front and back. In many earlier projects, the two-ness was the outgrowth of a sense of the role of building in the urban fabric, between the faces of public and private, a condition recursively explored within the working arrangements of the grouping itself. Of course, any architecture that wants to move begs the question of direction. If the classic modernist building embraced the metaphor of the ship, sailing along its long axis, Gehry has managed to disperse this sense of movement, to make a more general condition of animation. And here the metaphor of the flower grows again. The idea is the opposite of Muybridge's and seeks not to observe by retardation but by acceleration, in the kinds of time-lapse photography that, by speeding up the succession of images, makes the opening of a flower or the construction of a building freshly accessible.

Although the blooming and the building might fairly be said to proceed to certain ends, what Gehry, in his most recent work, has captured is not the directed motion but the stationary dynamism of a flame. The evanescence of the reflective facades of the Weisman Museum and the Guggenheim achieve the feeling of motion, not by the conceit of stop-time, like the Kobe fish or Vitra, but via literal animation. This fantasmagoria of moving light is not projected on a simple screen, like minimalist mirrored facades that try to garner meaning from sun and clouds, but on a surface that is itself complex. Bilbao surely marks the mature phase of Gehry's cubist sensibility, in which he returns cubist two-dimensional depictions of three-dimensional space to the actual realm of volume. It is a masterpiece.

39

40

then and now. As I came up through the ranks, Raphael Soriano was my model. Then I got excited about Japan, because my teachers at the University of Southern California had all come back from Japan at the time—and it really fit in Southern California. We got a pretty heavy dose of tatami mats, post-and-beam, and woodcraft structures. For me, it was in scale with what I could understand at the time. If you gave me a big building, I couldn't understand it. The all-time hero of that period for me was Harwell Harris. I knew him. I used to visit him in his studio. He practiced near downtown, up on a hillside on Mount Washington. I visited every month. Then I met Schindler. I was very taken with Schindler...then Neutra. I couldn't relate to him, but he liked me. I took my thesis project to his studio to show him; he said nice things and took a lot of time with me.

Rudolf M. Schindler
Schindler/Chase House, 1921–1922
West Hollywood, California

Richard Neutra
Lovell House, 1927–1929
Los Angeles, California

Craig Ellwood
Palevsky House, 1970
Palm Springs, California

Alvar Aalto
Paimio Chair, 1931
molded and bent birch plywood
The Museum of Modern Art,
New York, gift of
Edgar Kaufmann, Jr.

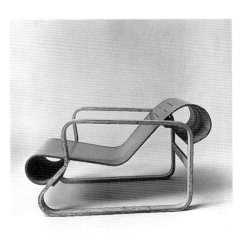

I was anti-Corbusier and all those people until I went to Harvard, and then I met a lot of them. But I didn't understand Corb. I had to go to Europe—see the Romanesque churches, go to La Tourette and Ronchamp—then I understood. Then I started into Frank Lloyd Wright—looking at it. That's what I used to do on weekends. When I came back from Harvard, I was driving across the country with my first wife and daughters, and I wanted to go to Taliesin West. I went to Taliesin and the flag was up, which meant that Wright was there. I was excited. I drove up, and they wanted a dollar each for us to go in, and I said, "No way." I was furious. I was a Socialist, and that offended me. So I didn't go in. I was always sorry.

commentaries by
frank gehry

When I was sixteen I attended a lecture at the University of Toronto, and a wonderful man from Finland showed a chair.[1] I remembered the lecture and later realized that the man was Alvar Aalto. I loved him. I loved the lecture. Then in 1972 Berta [Mrs. Gehry] and I went to Finland, and we visited Aalto's studio. They let us sit in his office for two hours. They let me sit in his chair. But I never met him. Then, years later, a lady came to my office. She looked familiar, but I didn't know who she was. She talked to me for an hour before I realized. I said, "You're Mrs. Aalto. He is my hero." What Aalto did for architecture is what I also like about Hans Scharoun. It's the touch,

[1] The chair in question was the Paimio (1931), named for the town and the tuberculosis sanitarium designed by Aalto (1929–1933). The character of its birch bent and laminated plywood construction undoubtedly had a lasting, if subliminal, influence on Gehry.

43

it's the humanity of it. Wright had that, too. I think Corb had it, but in a different way.

Painting and sculpture influence my work. For instance, when I had the Bellini picture with the Madonna and Child, I originally thought of it as the Madonna-and-Child strategy for architecture. You see a lot of big buildings with a lot of little buildings, little pavilions in front. I attribute that to the Madonna and Child composition. When I was doing some of the planning work for the Reichmans, for the Madison Square Garden proposal, I dragged out that Bellini picture and showed it to them. I showed it to the wrong people. I showed it to devout Jews, and they didn't want to hear about Christ. And I knew that. I told them, "I'm not trying to sell you Christianity, believe me, but there is a visual strategy that is built into the Judeo-Christian world that is Madonna and Child." I went back to the Bellini and fastened on the folds of the drapery. You see that kind of motion in Giotto, too. A lot of that folding interests me. I was looking for movement earlier, and found it in the fish. The fish solidified my understanding of how to make architecture move. The fish form that I designed for the Walker exhibition—I cut off the tail, cut off the head, cut off everything, and you still got a sense of movement—was really powerful for me. To have been able to build that was really important. Then I made a bigger one for Jay Chiat's Hampton Drive temporary offices [1986–1988]. The scale changed there. I made it more of a room, a communal room. I think my ideas are derived more from painting than sculpture. But I'm all over the place. You know, whenever I go to a museum I fall in love with something—Botticelli's *Primavera*, for example—but each time I see it differently from the last time. Today I would look at the fabrics. And I would see it architecturally, whereas I never saw it that way before. When I drive I'm listening to Proust now. I read Proust thirty years ago. I slogged through it; I wasn't ready. Now I just go nuts. I play it over and over. When he describes the town, when he describes the room, when he describes the hills, the sky. Now I'm listening to Trollope—*The Warden* and *Barchester County*. I hadn't read much of that earlier, but now I hear the descriptions of the parties, and they're architectural for me. I'm ready to hear it. I respond to where I am and what I'm doing at the time. You know you're given a problem, it has a context, it has a budget, it has people, and you start working with it. Then I draw from things that are appropriate that I relate to. Had I seen Claus Sluter [the fourteenth-century Flemish sculptor] ten or fifteen years ago, it probably wouldn't have resonated.

When I was working on Disney Hall I got excited about movement. I got into sails and the luffing of the sails. When you're sailing, the wind catches the sail and it's very tight, and it's a beautiful shape. Then, as you turn, the wind is coming at you when you're going forward—the wind is actually coming at an angle. When you turn into the wind slightly, the wind is on both sides of the sail. At that moment, the sail luffs—flutters. And when it flutters, it has a beautiful quality that was caught in the seventeenth century by Dutch painters such as the van de Veldes. But I didn't have the guts to do it. So everything is tight in Disney Hall. Later, when I saw Sluter, it was luffing all over the place; it was very much like

44

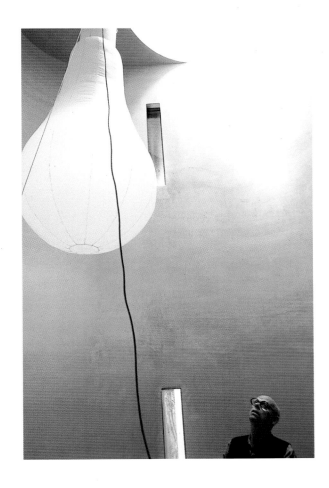

Claes Oldenburg in one of the
two binocular conference rooms,
Chiat/Day Main Street Headquarters, Venice, California, 1991

opposite:
Giovanni Bellini (1430–1516)
Madonna and Child,
oil on panel
Galleria Borghese, Rome, Italy

Claus Sluter (d. 1406)
*Mourner from the Tomb of
Philip the Bold*
alabaster, 16½ inches high
Cleveland Museum of Art
purchase from the
J.H. Wade Fund; bequest of
Leonard C. Hanna

elements from design process
models of the unrealized Peter
Lewis Residence, 1985–1995

Greek drapery. It gave me courage.

A number of artist friends have influenced my work. Ed Moses was a big influence on my life. He was somebody I learned a lot from, talked to a lot. I'm indebted to him. I learned a lot from Robert Irwin. I used to love meeting with him. I miss meeting with him. I miss our times together. Even though I didn't understand half the things he was saying, the intensity and the passion were really exciting to be around. Claes Olden-burg and Coosje van Bruggen are important to me. Claes is shy and difficult to get to know on his own. I think he's brilliant. Coosje talks more, and she is catalytic to a conversation be-tween us. Claes's work is about the figure, basically. When he did the binoculars, and he got that rolling surface and it was easy to build, I got excited.[2] But I didn't necessarily take that idea from him, because I was looking at Sluter, I was looking at Vermeer, I was looking at Bellini, and at Greek sculpture. I try things on, like I used to when I was a kid. I do it all the time. I get to know it. I assimilate it, and then it comes out some other way—translated.

I don't talk about influences when I give lectures, because my work doesn't look as good as Sluter, or Bellini, or Vermeer. Their work is better than my regurgitations of it. That's why I say I try it on, I assimilate it, and then it comes out some other way. No one would ever say, "Oh! Sluter," when they see my work.

[2] Oldenburg's binoculars, initially created for the Venice, Italy *Il Corso del Coltello* project (1984), were re-created by Claes Oldenburg, Coosje van Bruggen, and Frank Gehry for the Chiat/Day Headquarters building in Venice, California.

**Danziger Studio/Residence,
Hollywood, California, 1964**

**stucco detail,
Danziger Studio/Residence**

**opposite:
O'Neill Hay Barn,
San Juan Capistrano,
California, 1968**

materials and methods. They teach materials and methods in architecture school, as a separate course. I'm a craftsman. I took woodcraft classes when I was a kid, but I wasn't the greatest at it. My father had a furniture factory, and I used to help him. It seems to me that when you're doing architecture, you're building something out of something. There are the social issues, there's context, and then there's how do you make the enclosure and what do you make it with?

From the very beginning I've been worried about the translation of ideas through the many people involved in the process of making a building. They frequently drain the strength and power out of an idea. In my early attempts, such as the Danziger building, we ran into trouble at the building department, because it needed some kind of approval for the particular plaster spraying process I wanted to use. The building department didn't want us to do it. I've forgotten why. I remember they said, "Why don't you just do things the normal way?" I was conscious from about the time I was working on Danziger that you had to think of the finished building. So it became how you took the energy of the idea through the process and ended with a building that had feeling, genuine passion. The Danziger building had to be plaster. And I wanted a raw, rough texture. I was looking at Kahn a lot, but I was also looking at Corb. Whatever was in my consciousness, I loved raw rough stucco. No

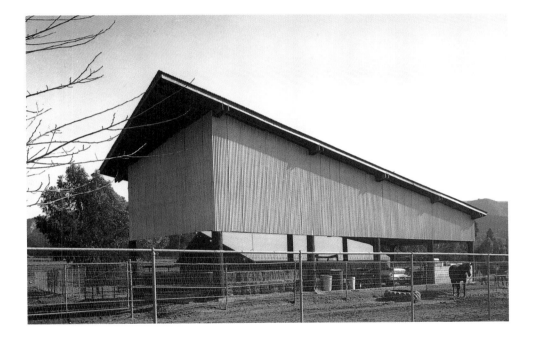

buildings were being done with that. They call it "tunnel mix." It was underneath the freeways. Under the freeways they'd spray it on. So I asked the plastering contractor to do it, and they said they couldn't; they didn't know how.

An artist friend was building a little studio in Venice. I told him what I was looking for. He said it sounded great, and if I wanted to use his garage to experiment on, he wouldn't mind. I found out what the equipment for tunnel mix was. I went to the U-Haul and rented it, mixed the plaster, and did it myself. I sprayed it on the garage, and it was beautiful! Then I brought the contractor down, showed him the equipment, showed him the walls, and that's how the Danziger building was made.

Since then—not because of me—you can only get tunnel mix! It's a totally perverse world.

When the sculptor Ron Davis wanted a studio, he bought land, and he came to me. I made the site model, and started to play with perspective. I made it so that it fit the site, so that the site and the building became a sculptural entity. I remember tipping the roof up, because I had done the hay barn for Donna O'Neill with a tipped-up roof. And he loved that. It was my first metal building after the hay barn. I said, "This is interesting for me, because I can now make a very tough sculptural shape." The wall and the roof became the same material, and we could do it in metal. That's when I started using corrugated metal.

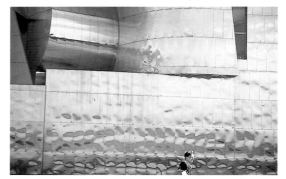

48

metal cladding has been a hallmark
of Gehry's architecture since the
late 1960s, from corrugated metal
to lead-coated copper to the more
esoteric titanium of Bilbao

I used metal to make three-dimensional objects. I explored metal: how it dealt with the light in Boston on the 360 Building, and in Toledo, where I used lead copper. The lead copper in Toledo is just beautiful. It does beautiful things with the light. The first time I used the metal pillow surface was on the Aerospace Museum. The big metal piece that hangs out is pillowed. I started out to do it otherwise, but I realized that you couldn't control it flat. Flat was a fetish, and everybody was doing that. I found out that I could use metal if I didn't worry about it being flat; I could do it cheaper. It was intuitive. I just went with it. I liked it. Then when I saw it on the building, I loved it. I used it again on Irvine. And then at Herman Miller I used it even thinner. Bilbao is a lot thinner because it's titanium. You couldn't use it the same thickness as the others—wouldn't be able to afford it. We prefer titanium because it's stronger; it's an element, a pure element, and it doesn't oxidize. It stays the same forever. They give a hundred-year guarantee!

I'm interested in Pop Art. However, that's not what moves my work, even though it is often misunderstood as that. When I was using chain link, people thought that was what I was doing. But it wasn't. The chain link for me was about denial. There was so much chain link being absorbed by the culture, and there was so much denial about it. I couldn't believe it. That's the populism in my work, as opposed to the art. What's wrong with chain link? I hate it, too, but can we make it beautiful? I said, "Maybe, if you make it beautiful, if you're going to use it in huge quantities, you can use it beautifully."

sculpture as architecture. My early work was rectilinear because you take baby steps.

I guess the work has become a kind of sculpture as architecture. It started with the Barcelona fish. And that was again intuitive. Why did I draw the fish in the first place? I did it because of the postmodern game. I said, "Okay, if you're going to go back, fish are three hundred thousand years before man, so why don't you go back to fish?" So I started drawing fish. And then they started to have a life of their own. I started to really look at fish. I began going to the library and looking at pictures of all the fish that were there, learning how the scales work. I looked at fish in ponds—the sense of movement fascinated me. The Greeks did it, and Rodin did it. I'm a strict modernist in the sense of believing in purity, that you shouldn't decorate. And yet buildings need decoration, because they need scaling elements. They need to be human scale, in my opinion. They can't just be faceless things. That's how some modernism failed. When it started getting used by the developers, it became faceless. It became a language that self-destructed. What was missing was human scale.

The wood fish I made for the GFT people in Italy was hokey, because it had a funny tail and fins. But when you stood beside it and you didn't get involved with the details, you had a sense of movement. That's when I did the fish for the Walker show. I said, "Okay, the tail and fins are hokey, so let's cut off the head, let's cut off the tail, and see how much of the kitschy stuff we can get rid of, and still get the sense of movement."

detail of the titanium-clad façade,
Guggenheim Museum Bilbao, 1997

opposite:
entry detail, California Aerospace Museum, Los Angeles, 1984

University of Toledo Center for the Visual Arts, 1992

detail, Frederick R. Weisman Museum, University of Minnesota, Minneapolis, 1993

façade detail, Der Neue Zollhof, Dusseldorf, Germany 1999

49

**sketch for the unrealized
Samsung Museum of Modern Art,
Seoul, Korea, 1995**

**Catia shaded surface study,
Telluride Residence, 1998**

**opposite:
three views of the office
taken in February, 1999**

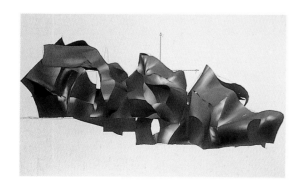

Even now I don't know where I'm going with it. Up to now the unbuilt Korean museum is the farthest out I've gotten. It's water. I was trying to make it water. I was trying to make a waterfall in Korea, because the most beautiful parts of Korea are nature. The man-made part is terrible there. So I was trying to relate to nature in Korea, and in the middle I was trying to make a waterfall. And I got close. There are a few places there where it works. I was getting close in a material way. In real life it would have started to be water, and I was really excited when they stopped it. But it's another sense of movement. It's liquid.

Then Jay Chiat's Telluride house goes the next step, which is indeterminacy—you don't know what the forms are. In other words, every time you look at it, it's going to be different. The models are ephemeral, and it's like ripping a piece of paper. The ripped edge can be beautiful. But you can't make architecture do that. I think I'm starting to explore that seriously in Jay's house. That indeterminacy that you get when you're not certain what it is. The Ron Davis house is a clear trapezoidal shape. You can read it, and you can remember it. Jay's house you remember as crinkled-up paper. Now, how do you get that into the final form? Water and crinkled-up paper: they're just another form of decoration in my opinion; in a way, it is baroque.

the new office. Our office structure and working method have changed a lot in the past ten years: staffing, computers, clients. It all has to do with people. Earlier, I could not get experienced managers and systems experts (the Randy Jeffersons and Jim Glymphs of the world) to work with me, because they could be paid better in other places where there was more predictability for them in their work and in their lives. People who worked here in the mid-1980s would freak out when I would redesign something, because that meant their bonus was out the window (if the client wasn't paying). That was the period when I ran into technical problems. We couldn't do working drawings for large projects; we had to farm them out.

When Jim Glymph joined us [in 1989] I pointed out that we drew curves like those on the Vitra Museum using descriptive geometry. I said, "I want to go into more complex shapes now." He said, "That's no problem; we'll do it with the computer." He went to the aerospace industry and had meetings and discussions about it. From those we got the Catia program and several new people, including the computer expert Richard Smith.

Jim developed the computer thing slowly, and that was expensive. But he does make it work for us. That's how we controlled the costs of Bilbao, and how we can do those curves now. Consequently, we have a lot of freedom. I can play with shapes. When I create the curved shapes on all the little models, we have a gadget that digitizes them. It's becoming quicker and quicker. With our new equipment, shapes can be transferred to the computer in fifteen minutes, and now we know how much it's going to cost per square foot to build those shapes, because we've had the necessary experience. Now we can budget jobs in the earliest design phases. Also, we know that if we use flat materials it's relatively cheap; when we use single curved materials it's a little more expensive; and it's most expensive when we warp materials. So we can rationalize all these shapes in the computer and make a judgment about the quantity of each shape to be used. It's not possible to know this by looking at the completed building. The most important thing is that the computer gives us a tool we can use to communicate with the contractors.

Because we can figure the cost, the subcontractors are starting to trust us. We have a whole group of people who know we mean it. At first, when they saw it, they thought we were crazy, and they said, "The client's not going to let you do it anyway, so why should we take it seriously?" Now they believe in it, and they want to be part of it. We have a large group of contractors in Europe and America who will work with us now. In the last few years we've been pushing the frontiers that we normally wouldn't push into, because we're afraid to do it! But there's a lot more flexibility out there than we realized.

When Bilbao came in we needed a great manager. Jim Glymph was here, but he isn't managerial. He's a technical genius. I thought we should look in the office and see if there was anybody we could grow into the position, but I said, "What I'd really like is Randy Jefferson." (I had been working with Randy on a house. He was Managing Partner of Langdon-Wilson, a big firm in downtown L.A.) Randy came by three days later, as though he had heard me.

Jim Glymph and Randy Jefferson have made the computer work for us. Bilbao looks like my drawings. When I saw it, I couldn't believe it. Jim figures it all out, and then he works with the contractors. Randy is different. He knows how to organize

the projects. So between them, it's a miracle. We're the only firm in the world doing what we're doing, and I think we're on the verge of revolutionizing the way architecture is practiced. Jim is starting to write software that other people will be able to use. I told them to go ahead and do it. They're meeting with the lawyers and the accountants. I've provided them with all the legal stuff. And I don't even understand it. You know it's not for me to do that. They're doing it. I'm going to stick to my thing. If they make a lot of money, that's fine. I may become the Bill Gates of architecture!

The new computer and management system allows us to unite all the players—the contractor, the engineer, the architect—with one modeling system. It's the master builder principle. I think it makes the architect more the parent and the contractor more the child—the reverse of the twentieth-century system. It's interesting because you wouldn't think that would happen with something as technical as the computer but, in fact, it has. And you wouldn't think an office like ours would lead it. Nobody else does it yet. But they will.

In Europe there's a person called the *metteur* who takes off the quantities of a building. We don't need him any more. The computer does that in an instant. So as we are designing the building, we have an instant *metteur* that takes off as we go. Consequently, I'm designing with specific conditions and I don't go out of bounds. Because you know, when you design without knowing the boundaries, you find a form and you become enamored with it. It crystallizes. It's a fixed image. It's really hard once it's a fixed image to go back and cut, cut, cut. But if you're cutting as you go, you don't get fixed until you know you can do it. When you're fixed, you're fixed. You know you can afford it.

Since we discovered the Catia software program we've worked with Dassault Systèmes in France, who makes it. In the last few years they've been working on making the system fit our way of working. So they now have a new enhanced Catia that they're going to install here, which backs us up even more and allows us to control the architectural processes to within seven decimal points of accuracy. That's what I like about it. They're tuned in to understanding that this can change the way architecture is practiced and can make new buildings possible—more exciting sculptural shapes in the landscape instead of just plain boxes. So they're excited about

that. I told them that I'm going to be perverse now and start doing boxes.

Bernard Charles, the President of Dassault Systèmes, has said that the way we're working has changed their way of thinking about their system, which is now having an impact on the way planes are designed. We're actually helping them in the aircraft and automobile industries.

project designers. I need to have help. I can't do it all myself. I've learned over the years how to assign work, how to get them going. Each person you work with is different, a different personality. They're not cookie cutters. If you try to make them the same, you destroy the dynamics of it. So it's more fun for me to play with their strengths and weaknesses. When I'm working on a project with Craig Webb, it's different from when I'm working on a project with Edwin Chan. If I give Edwin Chan a little sketch, he'll take it to the moon. By the time I get there, he's doubled the budget. And he doesn't care. He says, "Don't bother me with that kind of stuff." Craig Webb, on the other hand, is so facile that in thirty seconds he makes something look real. They're different, so I work differently with each of them.

Edwin is younger and he'll jump off a cliff without knowing it, and he tends to push things, which I love, because it pushes me. He was trained at Harvard. At the beginning he was very quiet and never talked, but now he talks, and if he doesn't like something, he says so. He has been here eleven or twelve years now, and he's not afraid of me. He's respectful, but he's not overly respectful. He has his own mind. Craig Webb was at Princeton. Craig is older, more experienced. When he draws something, it looks real. It's a trap for me sometimes; because he's so facile the project looks resolved. Edwin does not have the technical background, so when he draws an idea it is not resolved. When Craig does it it's buildable all of a sudden, and real; he'll take my sketches and play with them. Craig is overly respectful of me. He always thinks everything is going to go wrong. He's one of those guys who is sure that people aren't going to like something, or the budget is going to come in too high and the project's not going to get done. He's kind of a gloom-and-doom guy. Whereas Edwin's always up, always optimistic, always looking up, always smiling. They're my key designers right now.

bernard charles: There are many reasons we're interested in Gehry. For one: When you see what Frank is doing, the kind of architecture, the emotion he puts into it, when you look at it, you realize it hasn't been done before. Whether you like it or not is irrelevant. There is artistic power in the shapes. It's like the body. Today, what is new is not only that, it is the fact that he tries to be affordable. Planes and cars have a different logic to measure. For a plane, the measure is the cost of flying the plane. So it's related to the aerodynamics constraint and all those kinds of things. But in Frank's case, when he decided to use a certain type of steel he said, "This is the material I want." He is basically creating a shape, but he also has in mind the material he wants. He is saying to us, "Help me make sure that when I am going to create those shapes, I can still use this material." At the end of the day, he has made a shape, and if it's going to be extremely costly to produce because it's too expensive to bend, or because you have to stretch it, he is not going to be able to make it.

The computer is programmed in such a way that it knows what stainless steel can do. It knows what titanium can do, or what some other metal can do. You can even tell the computer, "Allow me this degree of freedom for what I can do with the material before it breaks," and the computer will tell you, "Oh, be careful here; you are going too far. This material will not resist or will not be okay for this shape." So you get interactive feedback. I believe no matter what shapes Frank can think of, with this process we can represent them. The dream that I have is to create the reality before it exists. And the other point is, as we all live in four dimensions—space and time—why should we restrict ourselves to working on a piece of paper?

a

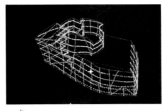

b

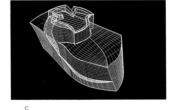

c

**the Catia process demonstrated
in a series of images of the
Guggenheim Museum Bilbao**

a Catia engineer tracing model for digital input
b digitized points form basis for 3D computer model
c surface model is created from digitized points
d shaded surface model is created
e CNC fabricated milled model is made to verify accuracy of 3D computer model
f primary structure for building is created
g secondary structure is created
h cladding pattern and 2D drawings are created from 3D computer model
i finished building

d

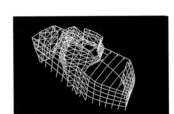

e

f

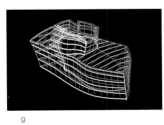

g

h

i

women in the office. Women in architecture schools are about fifty-fifty to men now. When I was a student it was about ten percent. Now I see a lot of women with real talent, raw talent, good talent. And you don't see them coming up in other offices, and I've wondered why. I talk about it in the office.

Eisenman sent me Rachel Allen, who is very, very bright, and very good. Eva Sobesky, who has been with us for a long time, is very bright and is working out really well. And then there is Michelle Kaufmann, who is working on Condé Nast and the Coca Cola Museum. Now we have five or six very promising women who can handle project management and design. I am encouraged. And I think a lot of it happens because of Berta, because Berta does her anthropological stuff in the office. She helps them. The women go to Berta, and talk to her. So I think I see hope.

contractors and architectural practice. The American legal system, the insurance system, and the tradition of the architect-client-contractor relationship are based on a bunch of phony assumptions. After the architect designs the building and does the drawings, he rises from the floor five feet and becomes the holier-than-thou arbiter between the client and the contractor. That's the assumption of the old system. What really happens is that the contractor goes to the owner and says, "If you straighten this wall out, I can save you a million dollars," and the client says, "Wow!" And sometimes he does it. The contractors, because of their relationship to the money, become parental in the equation, and the architect becomes the child—the creative one. "Here comes the creative one again; watch out."

The computer changes the system. We show the contractor the computer system and we show him a wall, built like the most difficult piece of the design. We also give him a disk that says "give this to the stonecutter. We want 1,700 pieces of stone double curved, 800,000 single curved, and 800,000 flat of this size." And the stonecutter says, "Oh, that's not a problem." He takes a look and says, "Flat is one dollar, single curve is two dollars, double curve is ten dollars," multiply that by the areas we give him, and he is happy. In fact we're doing a lot of the contractor's work. They're happy. They smile. They like it. Now the problem is the insurance companies. This being a system of legal responsibility, the lawyers say, "Wait a minute, you're opening yourself to all kinds of lawsuits." And the insurance company says, "Wait a minute, you're doing something different. We don't know how to insure this if you're going to take more responsibility." So it's complicated. But we're doing it anyway. We have insurance, but the cogs don't quite fit yet.

clients. I haven't been doing much developer work in America, because American developers are afraid of all the complications. But we're doing buildings in Germany for developers. The European client is more sophisticated than the American. It's tradition—the European tradition for architecture.

Working with the clients for the Experience Music Project in Seattle has been fascinating. Looking at a recent model (we make many as a project evolves) Paul Allen said, "I don't know

54

how you got from there to here.[3] I don't like here because it's not like what I liked. But I know that this is not an arbitrary effort. You did this for reasons I don't understand." So he invited me to explain it to him, and I did. That's what happens more or less in every client confrontation. They think I'm doing four different schemes. "I like the first one, the second one, I liked the third one—now you're doing it again?" So they think you're pulling the carpet out. Some clients don't understand the process. What I'm telling them is, "I'm bringing you into my process. Watch it, get involved, understand that I'm not stopping here." When I present this to them I explain where I'm going in words that human beings can

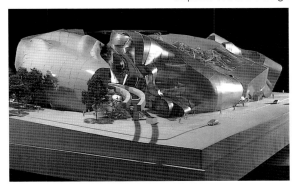

understand. I don't know where I'm going. I just explain the issues. Is it better not to do that? Is it better to come in at the end, and say, "This is it?" If the client doesn't feel married to the project, you're dead. If the client buys in, you're home free, because then no matter what happens the client will go along with you. My success has been that, and it makes for better buildings.

Architects are at the mercy of all the ups and downs of the economy and the demand for construction. That's why we have to change the way architecture is practiced, because architects take the blame for the market's ups and downs. If things go up and there's inflation, and you're working on a building, then the client will blame the architect. He's got to blame somebody, and so the architects are at fault. That's

why this system that we're using is a lot clearer, because we can tell them, "Okay, you want to take 10 percent out? This is what you get—a box—for 10 percent less. You can have this building with architecture, but if you don't want it, take away the architecture and build it yourself." The building is all set. We just don't want our name on it. You have an efficient building and it functions; you have a choice. And we tell them before it's too late.

Now, most architects pretend that there's no problem and they get the client "a little bit pregnant," and then it's too late, and then they get blamed, and the profession gets blamed for being a bunch of flakes. When you get a bid from a contractor, you can tell with our system whether or not it's an accurate bid if the drawings are complete. You have a legal document. If somebody bids $100 million on a job, and it's going to cost them $120 million, if the drawings are very complete, he loses $20 million. If the drawings aren't complete, he can really start asking for extras and jack up the price. That's what they usually do. But we are so accurate with the computer that they don't have any wiggle room, because we give them quantities, to seven decimal points of accuracy. It's that clean. It's really precise.

But still, when they bid, instead of saying "it's going to cost $10 to build this," they can say $20, and you can't really prove they're wrong. But there are some contractors we trust, for example, Massimo Colomban's company Permasteelisa, in Treviso, Italy. Colomban is an engineer in his forties. He bought the company that built the Sydney Opera House. He builds curtain walls for I.M. Pei, for Norman Foster, all over the world. He's ambitious. He made the fish in Barcelona and later the skin on Bilbao. He's a curtain wall expert. Jim Glymph and he struck up a good relationship, and we converted him to Catia. We talk to each other by modem. He's starting a plant over here, so he may start doing more of our work. He is building the Condé Nast cafeteria in New York. He'll put it on a boat, no problem. He'll build all the titanium, everything that has shape to it that has to be prefabricated. And it's cheaper to have him do it and ship it in than to do it in New York. The problem occurs when it has to be put together. That's where we get hurt in the millions. He will put it together, but we have to hire people in New York to stand by. They won't do anything. They'll just stand there and get paid for watching.

design process model of the Experience Music Project, Seattle, Washington, 1995

opposite:
Craig Webb, Edwin Chan, Frank Gehry in conversation with their design teams, May 1999

[3] Paul Allen, co-founder of Microsoft, is the client for the EMP, and one of Seattle's most beneficent citizens.

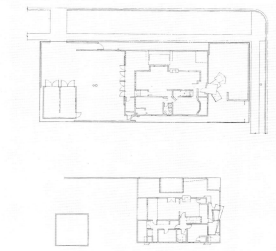

west façade of the renovated Gehry House, Santa Monica, California, 1992

opposite:
front entrance of the original Gehry House, 1978

the north façade of the renovated Gehry House with partial view of the garden and the kitchen window, 1992

changing our house. I'm kind of a realist. I don't hold anything that precious. Life is life, and we need to move on. The only thing I had trouble with was our house—changing it. I mean, that was a real scare, because whatever I did the first go-around couldn't be quantified, couldn't be talked about. I couldn't say, "This is what I was trying to do, and this is what I did." I started out to do something, and then I followed the end of my nose. The influences were from Joseph Cornell to Ed Moses to Bob Rauschenberg. I gathered up the visual knowledge to make the moves I did. When Arthur Drexler [4] came here for dinner one night, he thought the house was a joke. Berta told me afterward that he asked if the peeling paint was intentional. That's what was strong about it. What he was laughing about was what made it. You were never sure what was intentional and what wasn't. It looked in process. You weren't sure whether I meant it or not. There was something magical about the house. And I knew that the thing a lot of people hated or laughed at, was the magic.

Now twenty years have passed. Sami's grown up. When I did the first one, only Alejo was here; then came Sami. I decided on a nice room for Alejo and a nice room for Sami, and I started to do that, and it unraveled. [5] I couldn't be what I was twenty years earlier. I couldn't. I wanted the lap pool, and I wanted to make the garage a guesthouse for my daughters. So I started doing it, and I lost the old house! So it's caught in the middle. It's a hybrid. And I know I lost the old one. I know this isn't as good. The new house is every bit as comfortable as the old one, more comfortable. But it lost that edge. I could catch that freshness again with this new language. I just didn't have enough money to do it.

[4] Arthur Drexler was Director of the Department of Architecture and Design at The Museum of Modern Art in New York from 1956 to 1987.

[5] Gehry has two sons, Alejo and Sami, with his wife Berta, and two daughters, Brina and Leslie, from his first marriage.

the work

Abby Sher commissioned the Edgemar project. Her image was the towers of San Gimignano and a plan that would create a courtyard. There was an old egg factory on the property that she wanted to convert into a museum, and she had the Santa Monica Museum of Art group that wanted to be there. She wanted to do something special, of a communal nature. She also wanted it to make money.

If you make a shopping center, you have to have an anchor tenant that draws people in. In this case, the anchor tenant was going to be the museum. I said to her, "That's a precarious anchor tenant, because it's not a viable institution yet; you're just creating it." She also wanted a bookstore. She had fantasies about the kinds of things she liked, and they were all commercially naive. To her credit, she knew that. We'd talk about it, and she'd say, "Yes, but I think I can make it work. I've

**the ancient towers of
San Gimignano, Italy**

edgemar development 1984–1988
Santa Monica, California

got the critical mass, I've got the staying power, I can overcome those things with my resources." So the system I came up with was two forty-five degree angles, walkways into the courtyard. And the focus of it was the elevator, which I covered in chain link, making a sculpture out of it. That was one of the San Gimignano towers. Then in the front, I put in a couple of other towers.

She got a bunch of tenants, such as Ben & Jerry's Ice Cream. She got a dress shop in the front tower, and she started to lease space in the most unconventional way. She put a bookshop in the back. I said, "This stuff is just going to die." But somehow she made it work. She's had some turnover. To her credit, she's stuck to her guns. The museum is out now. She gave that space to a theater group run by some actors.

Edgemar is a small-scale commercial/art development on Santa Monica's Main Street. The project is one of Gehry's villagelike complexes arranged around a courtyard, consisting of five buildings and three tower structures in a variety of shapes and materials. A former egg factory, now a theater, has been modified and sheathed in copper and green-glazed tile. The ground floor of the curved building is covered in galvanized metal; the second floor is gray stucco. One tower is enclosed with chain-link mesh, one is a greenhouse structure, and the third is an open steel-framed irregular cube. The restaurant at the rear of the property is housed in two wood-framed former dairy structures.

61

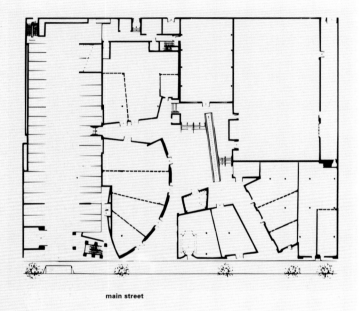

site plan

main street

edgemar development

64

**chain-link-mesh elevator tower
interior detail, and full view**

client: Sher Development

project principals: Frank O. Gehry, design principal
David Denton, project principal
C. Gregory Walsh, project designer
Sergio Zeballos, project architect

project team: Anne Greenwald,
Robert Hale, Rene Illustre,
David Pakshong, Randy Leffler,
Susan Narduli, Adolph Ortega,
Carroll Stockard, Roberta
Weiser, Sharon Williams

65

I owned the property where the project now stands. Fred Weisman, Greg Walsh, and I bought it together as partners.[6] We were going to convert the old Gas Company building into a museum, and then build studios for artists and commercial properties to pay for it. The people we bought it from owned the property on either side, and when they saw our plan they wanted to go in with us. So they were going to include their property in this thing, and we were going to do the whole thing as one piece. But the Coastal Commission and the Venice community turned down our plan. They didn't want artists' studios. They wanted low-cost housing. It was a movement in Venice and Santa Monica led by Tom Hayden. We were really shot down by the community, really abused. It was absurd. So when we lost that, Fred lost interest; he didn't want to do it. So we sold the Gas Company building. We were left with an L-shaped parcel, and we now had it for free, because what we sold the building for paid for the rest. So now Fred, Greg, and I were partners on a piece of property, and the Coastal Commission wouldn't let us do anything with it. I wanted to build small shops. Everything we came in with got killed. It was high profile stuff, and they were out to get us. We couldn't sell it. Fred wanted to take it over, and I didn't want to give it up. It was the only thing I owned that was worth anything. He suggested that I should buy it from him. I had to come up with the money, so I traded all my art for the land.

During that time I was doing the Wosk House [1982–1984], and Miriam invited us to the Hollywood Bowl to hear the Israel Philharmonic. She had a friend with her, Jay Chiat, whom I had never met. We talked, and he told me that he was looking for land. He wanted to move his offices. He said he wanted to build, and he was looking for an architect; would I consider doing it? I said, "Sure." I asked him where in Venice he was looking. It didn't occur to me to tell him about my property. Because he asked me to do a building, I felt, "I can't hustle him to sell my land." I thought, that's too much. So I said, "Call me when you get a piece of land, and I'll go look at it with you." So a few weeks passed and he called me, and he said, "You know, the realtor tells me you own a prime piece of land, and it's perfect for what we want. Why didn't you tell me?" I said, "Because..." Anyway, long story short, he bought it from Greg and me.

By now, the political climate had changed and we were

chiat/day
main street headquarters 1985–1991

Venice, California

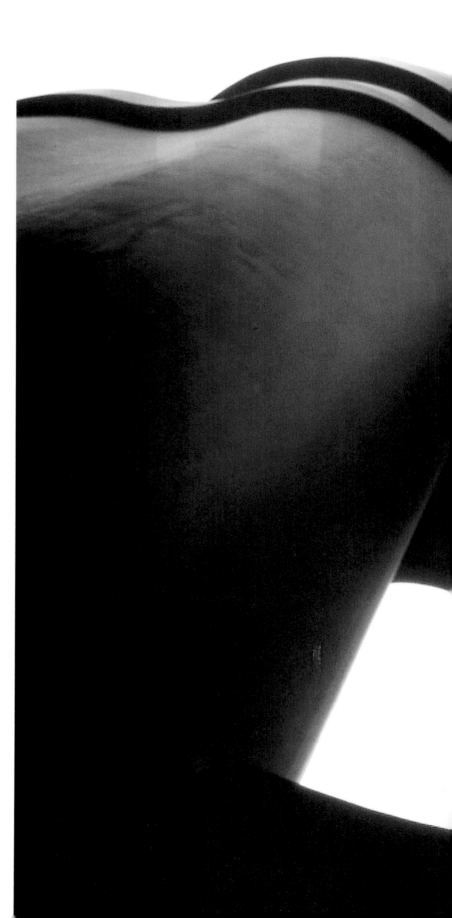

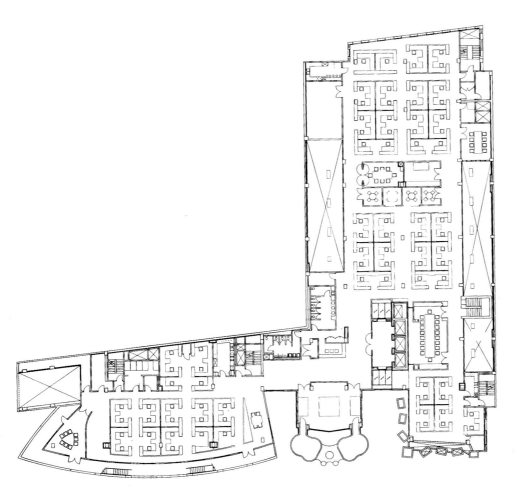

previous page:
detail of the binocular façade

opposite:
**copper clad-columns and beams
on the Main Street façade**

second floor plan

68

6 Fred Weisman, now deceased, was a well-known art collector and long time Gehry client; Greg Walsh is an architect who practiced with Gehry for many years.

7 Camp Good Times, an unrealized project, was a collaboration between Claes Oldenburg, Coosje van Bruggen, and Frank Gehry for a summer camp for children with cancer, to be located in the Santa Monica hills.

able to go ahead with a building. When they started digging, they discovered toxic waste, and it delayed everything for more than two years.

We started with a three-piece structure, and I was working very hard designing each piece as a separate element. I had sketched ideas of what it would be, but they were just vague sketches. I had designed brick turrets. I had an idea for a brick castle with turrets in the middle. I had the two sides pretty well started, then Jay got impatient and said, "What are you going to do in the middle?" I had a little box with a pin cushion stuck on it that looked like a train coming out at you. He said, "You're not going to do that, are you?" I said, "No." I had the lit-

tle binoculars of Claes Oldenburg on my desk, the red ones that we'd used in the Venice performance piece, *Il Corso del Coltello,* in 1984. Jay kept pushing me and they were within reach. I took them and put them there. I said, "Okay, it's something like this." He said, "Would he do it?" I asked, "What do you mean, would he do it?" He said, "Would Claes do it?" I said, "I don't think so. They are very fussy about context, so I don't know."

We had been working together on Camp Good Times,[7] and Claes and Coosje had been juxtaposing objects, and the binoculars were something we'd worked on together. I told Claes what happened, and I said, "I'll understand if you don't

want to do it, but just look at it." So we sent all the pictures to Claes and Coosje, and they loved it. Then they started working on it, and made it beautiful. I got into it as part of the building. It seemed so right. I helped them with the construction of it, how to do it, and got it built as part of the building. At that time there were many symposiums about art and architecture collaborations, and nobody was really doing anything. So this looked pretty interesting to me. I had heard the public artist Siah Armajani talking about how artists are always in the background, and I thought it would be interesting to see what would happen if an artist were really a part of the building process.

We had all the interiors designed by ten artists. We had Kenny Price doing the bathrooms and Billy Al Bengston doing the carpets. It was going to be a major thing. Mike Kelly did two conference rooms. But Jay had to cut back, and he told me, "Look, I can't do it." So the interiors are not what they were going to be. They straightened up and just shriveled up. That happens a lot. We've tried a couple of things with artists since, but none has worked out. The client has to want to do it. It's an expensive thing. Jay was willing. He was a great client.

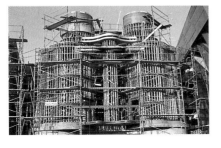

The 75,000-square-foot, three-story office building has three levels of parking below grade, entered through the Oldenburg/van Bruggen binoculars, which are also the main entrance to the building's ground floor. The binoculars, which contain conference rooms on two levels, are the building's central element, surrounded on one side by a curved stucco screen facade and on the other by copper-clad columns and tilted beams. Both exterior walls are designed to provide shade from the afternoon sun. The interior office spaces are lined with built-in plywood work areas.

binocular design process models and binoculars under construction

client: Chiat/Day Advertising

project principals: Frank O. Gehry, design principal
David Denton, project principal
C. Gregory Walsh, project design
Claes Oldenburg, Coosje van Bruggen, binocular design
Craig Webb, Clive Wilkinson, project architects

project team: Alan Au, Gerhard Auernhammer, Perry Blake, Thomas Duley, Anne Greenwald, Robert Hale, Victoria Jenkins, Alex Mecom

A design for a tract house was commissioned for an exhibition by the Leo Castelli gallery downtown. I did the tract house as a group of pavilions, and Marna Schnabel, who worked for me then, built the model. She came to me afterwards and said, "I love that house; will you build it for me?" We started to do the house that way, but it didn't work—the Schnabels' program was too big. So I concocted this other one. The tract house exhibition never happened. They turned it into a folly exhibition.

When you say the word "deconstruction" and you look at this house, you think the term fits. But it's just an opportunistic interpretation, because it was never done intentionally. I think the Schnabel house relates to Romanesque churches I was looking at. From the outside it looks California vernacular.

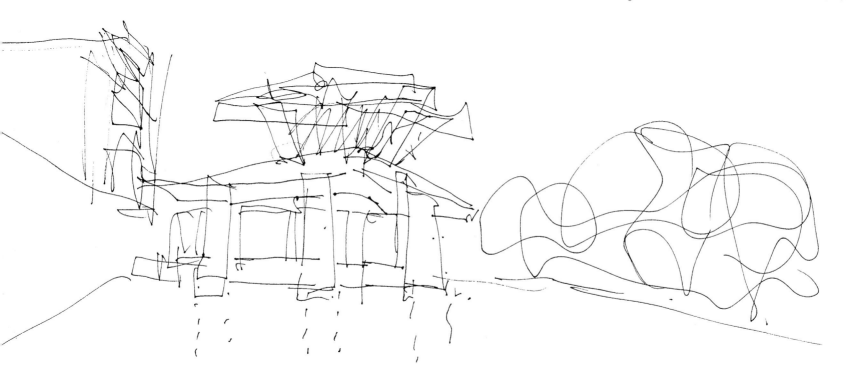

the schnabel house 1986–1989
Brentwood, California

This 5,700-square-foot collection of objects in a landscape is another of Gehry's distinctive, villagelike assemblages of the mid-1980s. The disparate character of each building reflects the diversity of the client's programmatic requirements. Lead-coated copper sheathes the central cruciform structure housing the living and dining rooms, library, kitchen, family room, and two bedrooms. The garage, topped by stucco-walled staff quarters, is at the front of the site. The upper garden includes a guest apartment, a lap pool, and an office/bedroom crowned with a copper sphere. The master bedroom pavilion sits on the edge of a shallow lake (lately converted to grass) at the bottom of the two-level garden.

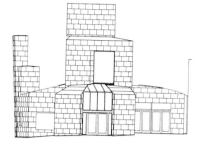

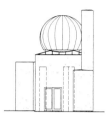

the schnabel house

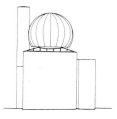

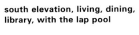

south elevation, living, dining, library, with the lap pool

opposite:
west entry walk

75

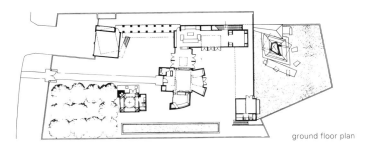

ground floor plan

client: Marna and Rockwell Schnabel

project principals: Frank O. Gehry, design principal
David Denton, project principal
C. Gregory Walsh, project design

project team: Tom Buresh,
Devin Daly, Rene Illustre,
Adolph Ortega, Carroll Stockard,
Sergio Zeballos

**master bedroom and
reflecting pool**

**opposite:
detail of living room skylights**

A long time ago, Max and D. J. DePree interviewed and hired us.[8] They asked us to associate with a local architect, which we did, and we liked them. We went through studies to do the ultimate assembly line computerized factory. We had a lot of meetings and we were working on a factory with a manufacturing system. Then, all of a sudden they decided that was not what they were going to do; they were going to build more of a warehouse facility. They were going to have production, but it was going to be assembly rather than major production, and they wanted "people places."[9]

They made a big deal about the people places. But in all the buildings they showed us, the people places never were built because they ran out of money. The reason they ran out of money was that the architects would spend so much on the high-tech skin of the factory that the people places were cut. So I was determined to do both. And that's when I called Stanley Tigerman and invited him to design a little theater, a simple building. With that and the copper-clad, trellislike pergola, we created an urban place.

herman miller, inc. western regional
manufacturing and distribution facility 1987–1989

Rocklin, California

© Yukio Futagawa

8 DePree family members were the owners and officers of the Herman Miller company in its early, most creative years.

9 The company uses the Scanlon Plan, which involves a number of humanistic programs for its employees, and a share in company profits.

view of the copper-clad pergola

opposite:
detail of the galvanized
steel-clad arcade

80

82

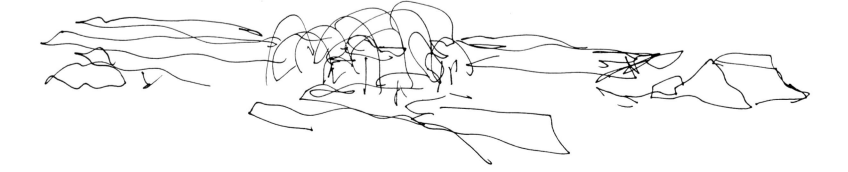

herman miller

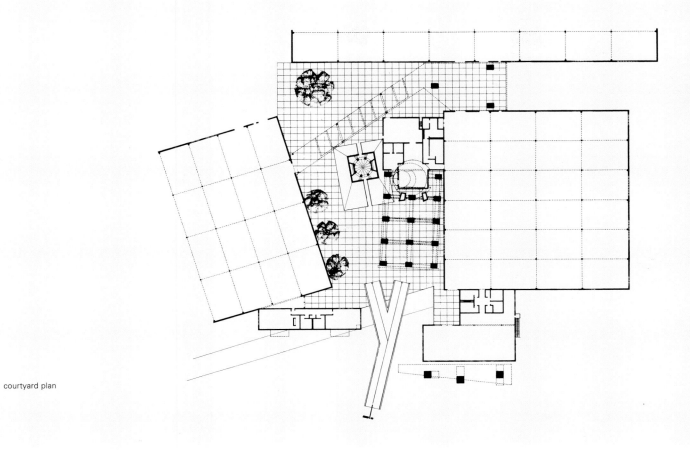

courtyard plan

Herman Miller's western plant is located near Sacramento, on a 156-acre site. Separate warehouse, assembly, and processing buildings, each about 100,000 square feet, are sheathed in flat galvanized steel siding and are functionally indeterminate to accommodate changing needs. In addition there is a 14,000-square-foot common space topped by a copper-clad pergola—a gathering place for employees that includes kitchen, lunchroom, meeting areas, and an audio-visual room designed by Stanley Tigerman. Tigerman's small neoclassical, silver-domed building sits in the public piazza—an odd though friendly neighbor to Gehry's dramatic volumes arranged along a rock-covered berm.

opposite:
**view of employee cafeteria
within pergola**

client: Herman Miller, Inc.

project principals: Frank O. Gehry, design principal
Robert Hale, project principal
Sharon Williams, project architect
Tom Buresh, project designer

project team: Edwin Chan,
Susan Narduli, Patricia
Owen, Berthold Penkhues,
Caroll Stockard

I love it from the freeway. Eight hundred feet of green stainless steel. We didn't do the inside except the stairway and the elevators. The challenge was to acknowledge the character of the client without succumbing to Disney cuteness.[10]

They didn't want to build it because it wasn't an income producer. It was just for their offices. So they didn't want to spend the money on back-of-house offices. They didn't need it as they were renting space all over the place. But the pressure on them to consolidate became pretty big. They delayed it for three or four years. Finally they said, "Go," and we built it for sixty dollars a square foot. It was very cheap. I don't think you could ever do it again. But it's a very efficient building.

The building was to be the most efficient building we could make. They gave me the freeway location. I really questioned being there, because they're building a second gate, and I thought that was the first place on the freeway where you could look into the site, and if we had been there, I would have opened a path and made a big deal about the second gate. But they didn't do that. So then I decided to make a freeway building that you would see going sixty miles an hour. It moves with you, and there's some sound with the cowcatcher base on the freeway side. On the other side, the building is open to Disneyland.

I was just starting to make curving shapes then. And at the point we were doing it, we thought Disney Hall wasn't going to be built. Just as Disney Hall folded, we were redesigning that exterior, so it was normal to use those shapes. That's why it's such a shame that they did nothing on the inside. The shapes came out beautifully. I love them.

A drawing of Goofy was blown up and laid onto an elevation of the stairwell. It's on different pieces of the pre-cast stair, so it appears to be segmented. We did the elevators, too, and they're a variety of exotic marbles. Then from then on they wouldn't let us do anything inside. They did the same thing to Arata Isozaki in Florida. It is the same program. They didn't let him do the interiors either.

ground floor plan

team disneyland
administration building 1987–1996

Anaheim, California

This 330,000-square-foot office/auditorium/cafeteria complex houses the staff that manages nearby Disneyland. The four-story office building bordering the freeway is clad in blue-green quilted stainless steel sheet metal; the park side is brilliant yellow-painted stucco in a series of curvilinear sculptured forms. Galvanized metal canopies indicate entranceways. The main entry interior stairway is a curved volume on which an image of Goofy is painted black on vivid pink walls. The exterior walkway connecting the buildings has a two-tone pattern of curved concrete stripes.

[10] From *Architecture*, July 1996.

entry façade on the park side,
painted stucco

freeway façade, quilted stainless-
steel panels

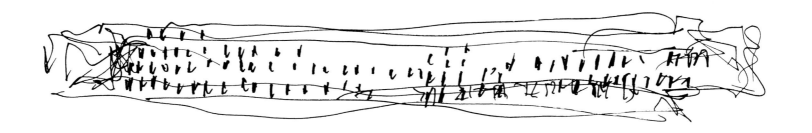

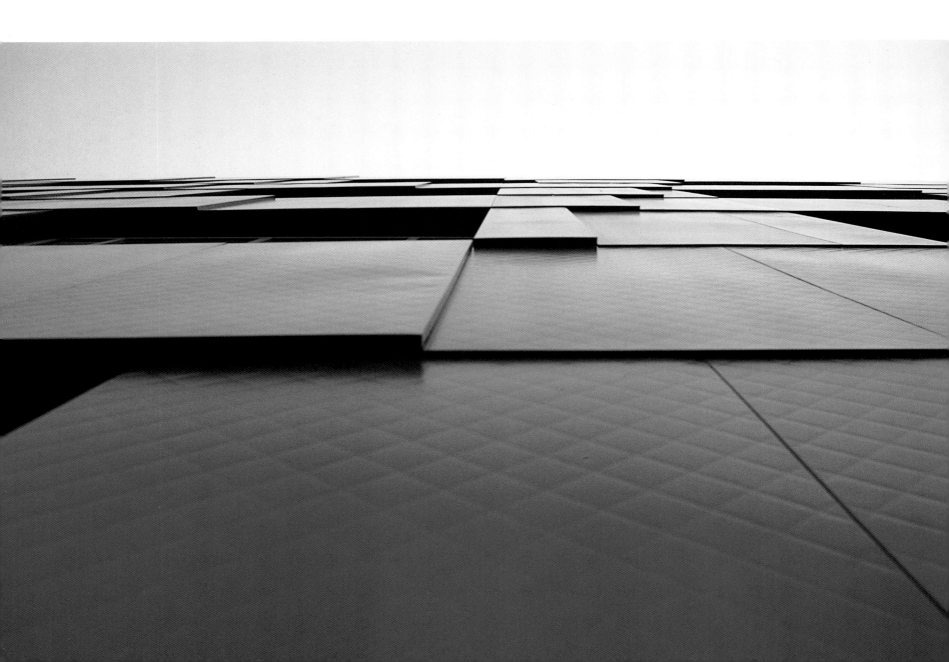

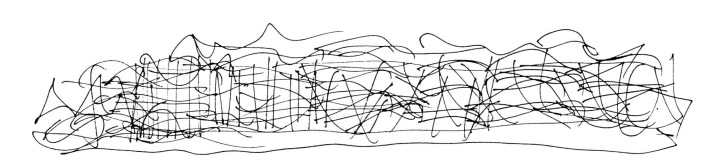

design process models

team disneyland, administration buildiing

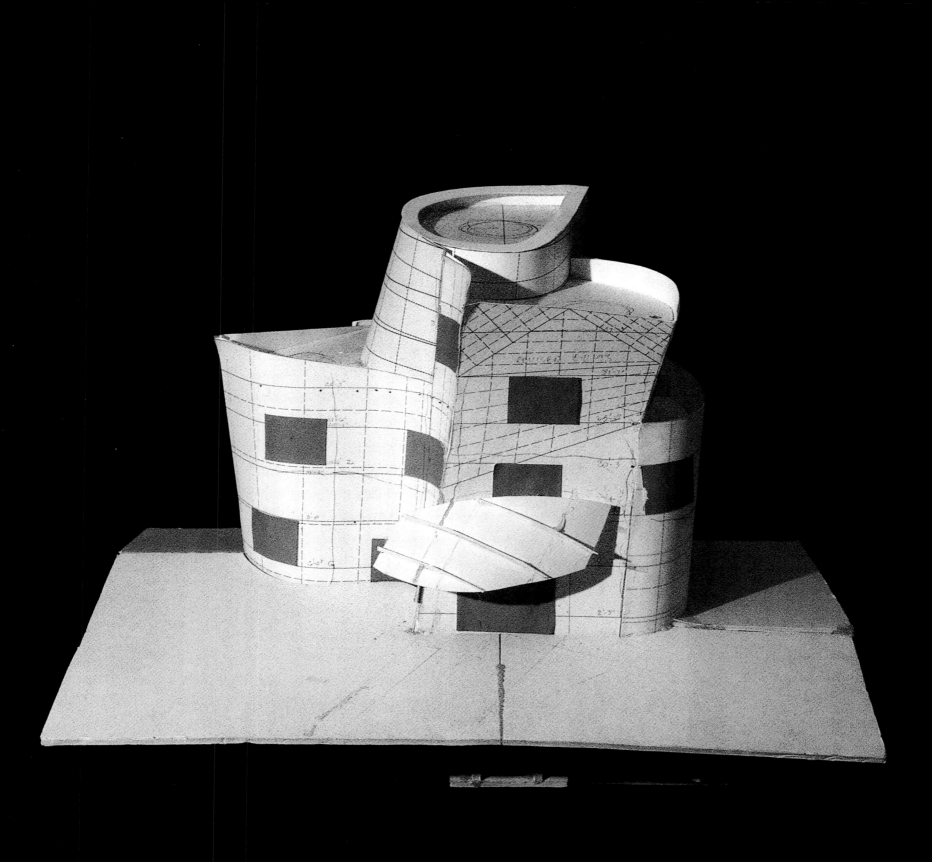

team disneyland, administration buildiing

lobby stairway under construction

opposite:
three views of the lobby
stairway with segmented
painted image of Goofy

client: Disney Development Company

project principals: Frank O. Gehry, design principal
Randy Jefferson, project principal
Bruce Biesman-Simons, project architect
Edwin Chan, project designer

project team: Kevin Daly,
Jonathan Davis, Jim Dayton,
David Gastrau, Robert Hale,
Patricia McCaul, Michael Resnic,
Todd Spiegel, Randall Stout,
Lisa Towning, C. Gregory Walsh,
Tim Williams

For several years, Rolf Fehlbaum [CEO of Vitra] wrote asking me to design a chair for him. I never answered him, because I didn't know how to go to Switzerland and design a chair. So I just put the letters in my "To Do" file. Over time they piled up. Then I got a call from Claes Oldenburg and Coosje van Bruggen; they were doing a sculpture for him. And they asked me to come and meet him, because they liked him, and they thought we'd get along, and I should do a chair for him. I told Claes that for me to do a chair I'd need to set up a little shop and have all my stuff, and I can't do it. Anyway, I was in New York once having dinner with Claes and Coosje, and they snuck in Fehlbaum. We met, and then he asked me to do the chair and I told him the same thing. It's like all these shows and things, I just say, "Yes, yes, yes, maybe someday," and then I never do it. Later, Claes and Coosje and I were in Milan, doing a class at the Polytechnique. Claes was installing the *Tool-Gate* and I went with them up to Vitra.

I got to know Rolf a little bit, and then several months passed and he called me. He said he was going to build a furniture museum. The *Tool-Gate* was a present for his father's birthday, and the museum was going to be a present for his mother. It was a tiny little workshop kind of museum he had in mind for exhibits of special chairs. He only had 200 chairs in the collection when we started. He thought he needed one room for a rotating collection, and then he'd have a room where he'd hold interior systems symposiums, so he wanted two galleries.

view of museum's main entrance (left) and the factory (below)

**opposite:
roofscape**

vitra **furniture museum and factory** 1987–1989

Weil am Rhein, Germany

vitra furniture museum and factory

I told him I couldn't do it from Los Angeles because the project was too small, and the fees would be outlandish for him—I thought he should get a local architect. He said, "We're going to build a big factory with it." I said, "Well, if you can see your way clear to letting me design the whole thing. The factory can be just a box, but it would work." He liked that idea, so we did the factory.

He had a lot of pleasure with the design of the museum, and it became exuberant. He felt that people going into the factory would be shortchanged if they didn't have a nice entrance. So the sculptural entrances to the factory started to happen, and I started playing with something that I was interested in, which was the urban quality that I could create out in the field, the urban quality between the museum and those entrances.

I was also interested in the play between my building and Nicholas Grimshaw's earlier high-tech factory, and I didn't want to preempt Grimshaw's high-techness. I thought it was good that he maintained that, and that I should either go way out forward or, well, I didn't have the money to go way out forward with the factory, so I just cut big holes in the walls, and it looked like an old-fashioned factory. When it was built, the factory part looked like it was there before Grimshaw's.

Many years later Rolf asked me to do the next factory, and I suggested Alvaro Siza do it, which he did. (That was after Zaha Hadid's firehouse was built.) And Siza, without telling anybody, did a brick factory, so his looks like it was done before mine. He was consciously doing it without saying it to us. It really works. When you go there you think, Siza, Gehry, and then Grimshaw.

Located in a rural area just across the border from Basel, Gehry's Vitra Museum and an adjacent factory are his first realized European projects. The museum is a unique work of art whose stunning, light-filled spaces serve a growing collection of industrially produced chairs and an expanding exhibition program. Undoubtedly inspired by two nearby landmarks, Rudolf Steiner's Goetheanum and Le Corbusier's Ronchamp pilgrimage chapel, Gehry has created a series of white plaster galleries, each with a distinctive spatial character. The building's white exterior is plaster over masonry with zinc roof panels.

97

vitra furniture museum and factory

museum installation with Gehry's
Little Beaver chair and ottoman
(1979) at right

opposite:
installation views

overleaf:
details of skylight interior and
exterior (opposite)

client: Rolf Fehlbaum, Vitra International, Ltd.

project principals: Frank O. Gehry, design principal
Robert Hale, project principal
C. Gregory Walsh, project designer
Berthold Penkhues and Liza Hansen, project architects

project team: Christopher
Joseph Bonura, Edwin Chan

  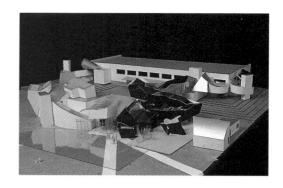

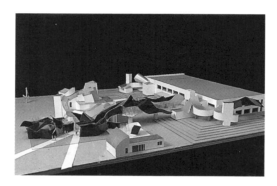 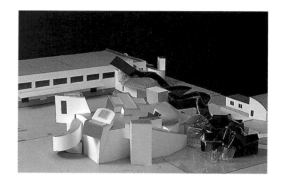

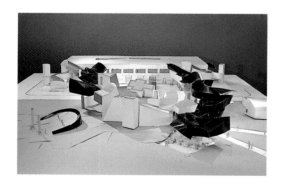 

addition to
the vitra museum 1998–

edwin chan: I don't think we've ever done this before—added to a Gehry building that has a specific sculptural presence. The issue is this: When we first designed the original museum it was only going to be a little family-run chair collection. Rolf Fehlbaum has done an amazing job in terms of managing, nurturing, and programming it. When I was there with Frank about a month ago, it was packed with people. The fact is it's not a chair museum and it's not a personal thing any more. Now it's a real design museum. So he wants to upgrade it in a way that will give him more programming flexibility, and give him more exhibition spaces. The other thing about this building is that the entrance was designed for his personal use, so there were no public amenities. No queuing spaces, no place for people to buy tickets and that kind of thing. So we want to solve this problem with the new entry.

It's hard to tack on to this building because it's very complex. So originally, we proposed an underground gallery with a skylight. The Louvre approach. You would go down to an underground gallery. The other thing Fehlbaum wanted to do was to figure out a way to connect to the factory building. The reason

for that is that on the second level of the factory building he has a nice showroom, and if we figure out a way for him to connect to the factory, then he can use the showroom as part of the museum program. So we have to figure out a way to do a bridge.

When Frank met with him in Berlin he challenged us to be a little bit more aggressive about it. He wanted something that has more sculptural presence. So instead of going underground, we will make an object in the front. We will develop that whole area into an entry with a bookstore and a café—a real lobby.

aerial view of the site model, including addition, 1999

**opposite:
series of process models, 1998–1999**

michael sorkin

This is a place not only for administrative offices, it is also for people who come to see furniture displays. Rolf Fehlbaum also wanted us to explore what the office of the future might be.

I did a lot of research on the office of the future, agonized about it, and gathered information. One day I was walking through the offices in the factory building we designed for Vitra, and I happened on a little room. I looked in; it was just beautiful, it was elegant—a table and a few things on the wall. I said, "You know, Rolf, with all this stuff about what an office should be, look, here's a guy who lives in his office; it's comfortable; there's something nice about it." And Rolf started laughing. It was Charles Eames's own office.[11]

So I had to make an office building and a conference center. I made the conference center with a café. The entry building was the sculpture. The office building was much simpler. That way the clients who came wouldn't say, "Well, look, your furniture looks great in this funny sculptural thing, but we have ordinary buildings." We didn't want to do that. So we made a bar building, and the sculpture sits in it, is kind of embraced by it, and the master plan has to have another bar building eventually. Then we made a basement, and the basement offended me there, so I opened it up and he rented out the basement, and it made a big difference in the economics of the building for him.

We've never done a chair for him. I don't know why. You can't trust me. I really love the Vitra Headquarters Building. I've painted the asphalt blue in front of the entrance. I call it the company swimming pool.

104

vitra international
headquarters 1988–1994

Birsfelden, Switzerland

Just outside of Basel, Vitra's 62,000-square-foot headquarters building is Gehry's addition to a planned development that includes two earlier structures. The headquarters office block includes areas in which demonstrations of new products take place, both traditional office furnishings and so-called office landscapes. The sculptural half of the building, called "the villa," is designed to fit comfortably with the homes nearby. The structural materials are similar to those at the Vitra Museum, and the two parts of the building are tied together via an undulating metal roof.

opposite:
view of villa (right), and office (left)

[11] Vitra has manufactured Eames
furniture in partnership with
Herman Miller for many years;
after Ray Eames's death the
company purchased the con-
tents of the Eameses' Venice
office, including Charles's office
furnishings. The Eameses'
archives were left to the Library
of Congress.

overview of final design model

vitra international headquarters

108 **conference rooms**

vitra international headquarters

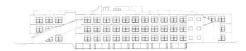

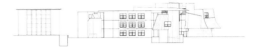
east and west elevations

north and south elevations

client: Rolf Fehlbaum, Vitra International, Ltd.

project principals: Frank O. Gehry, design principal
Robert Hale, project principal
Vince Snyder, project designer/architect

project team: Jim Glymph,
Liza Hansen, Peter Locke,
Eva Sobesky, David Stein,
Randall Stout, Laurence Tighe,
Dane Twichell, Brian Yoo

109

the american center 1988–1994
Paris, France

I wanted the project to be a *petite ville,* just like the city, full of music, activity, and energy. I tried to make the central space an open space, so that from there you could go to the movie theater, the main theater, the restaurant, and you would have been able to go into the book shop and travel agency. Then the loft space made sense as a kind of living room sitting in the middle of the space. The gallery is way up at the top, because that was the only place I could put it to get top light. The theater, which was inspired by Hugh Hardy's Joyce Theater, works extremely well.

dance studio

lobby atrium with the mezzanine lounge at its center

opposite:
400-seat theater

The American Center, a Paris institution devoted to American avant-garde art since its beginnings in the 1930s, was originally housed in an old building on Montparnasse's Boulevard Raspail. In the mid-1980s the directors decided the Center would become a part of the newly redeveloped Bercy district, across the Seine from France's new National Library. Using the proceeds from the sale of its building, the Center started down the rocky road that led to the eventual dissolution of the institution and the sale of its new home.[12] Covered in French limestone, the 198,000-square-foot building fits comfortably into its surroundings. Its street-side facade has a simple, quiet surface. The park side is energized by a series of lively, curving forms, and a swooping zinc-coated awning covers the main entrance. "The building is like a ballerina, lifting her skirt to welcome people into the building."[13] The complex program led to a very tightly organized interior in which Gehry attempted to provide the incredibly diverse spaces requested by the Center's planning committee. As the architect points out, the building's handsome 400-seat theater is undoubtedly its most successful element.

[12] In 1998 the American Center sold the Gehry building to the French Ministry of Culture. After some remodeling, it will become the Maison du Cinema, a film library and theaters, to open in 2000.

[13] From an interview with Gehry in *GA Architect 10,* 1993.

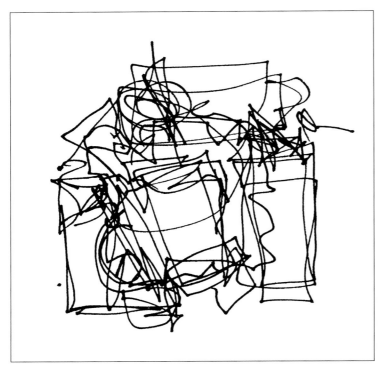

the american center

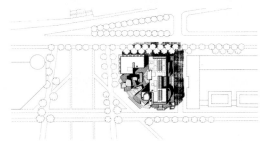

main entry

opposite:
view of the completed
building seen as an integral part
of its Bercy neighborhood

113

the american center

design process models, 1988

client: The American Center

project principals: Frank O. Gehry, design principal
Robert Hale and James Glymph, project principals
Thomas J. Hoos and Marc Salette, project architects
Edwin Chan and C. Gregory Walsh, project designers

project team: Kevin Daly,
David Gastrau, David Pakshong,
Brian Yoo

Euro-Disney is a maverick in my work. I think the thing I did wrong there was not doing the interiors and all the Mickey Mouse stuff. I said, "I can't do that." But I think I would have made the building come off if I had done it. It would have been a consistent thing. I didn't realize that I could become themed, but I was.

I talked to Claes [Oldenburg] a lot, and Claes said, "Don't do it." He said, "They'll co-opt you; don't do it." I said, "No, they just want me to be myself." Mine was the only building without a literal theme.

Everybody at Disney loved what I was doing. There are two things I don't like. One is that if you've seen everything else, my building becomes a theme in itself, because it's the only one out there. It's a de facto theme. They put restaurants in my building, and stores, and themes galore. And they asked me to do them. They said, "Why don't you do them—the 50s diner and all that stuff?" I said, "I'll do them my way, but not themes." The second thing was that I didn't realize the power of Mickey. You can't win. You could build 100,000 square feet, and if you put one life-size statue of Mickey in it, it's like a lightning rod. It takes up all the energy, because the world recognizes Mickey. There's a kind of spaceship on a pedestal in the courtyard. Mickey is sitting in it. I learned a lesson there. It was my fault, because they offered it to me and I was holier than thou. Claes was right.

view of the nightclub (foreground), food court and retail area (background)

opposite:
"Mickey" in a spaceship; a powerful image at the courtyard entrance

entertainment center, euro-disney
(now called **disneyland paris**) 1988–1992

The Marne Valley, near Paris, France

At the crossroads of the hotel area and the incoming transportation systems (the TGV inter-European train and the RER Paris Metro) at Euro-Disney, the Entertainment Center houses a collection of shops, restaurants, bars, discos, and a theater that features a Wild West show. The 185,000-square-foot structure is a combination of poured concrete and laminated wood columns covered in diagonal patterns of gold and silver stainless steel, zinc, and painted metal. A canopy of tiny white lights defines the space beneath the night sky.

client: Euro Disney, S.C.A.

project principals: Frank O. Gehry, design principal
Robert Hale, project principal
Bruce Biesman-Simons, project architect
Vince Snyder, project designer

project team: Andy Alper,
Gaelle Breton, Marc Salette,
Michael Sant

**tiny white lights create a
canopy in the night sky**

I loved doing the bentwood furniture—having the little shop and playing with it. But nobody wants to do that now. Marshall Cogan, who was running Knoll then, did. When he came to ask me to do the furniture, he said, "We'd like you to design a chair for Knoll," and I said, "It's really nice of you." But I said, "It's not going to happen." Then he said, "Why?" I said, "Well, the only way I can work is if I have a little shop and I can go there on my coffee break and I can play for an hour, and I do it every day, and at the end of two weeks you have something." He said, "Okay, rent the space, do it." Within six weeks I had the idea.

Cross Check is not the best chair.[14] I did one like it that's better, without the solid seat. But they never built it because I finished it a week after production started, and they wouldn't add it. I did a bunch of others. Lots of better ones. The principle of all of this was bushel baskets. The idea of making a table out of baskets was not very sensible, but they insisted I have a table, so I made one.

Making furniture is about production techniques. I always have to invent the whole production process, as I did for the cardboard furniture. For Knoll, too, we had to invent the whole thing. And once it got started, none of what we wanted to do passed all the rules and standards. Some of it was practical and some of it wasn't. But my sense was that we were going to make a big sheet of plywood as wide as this room, and bend it into the desired shape, and then run it through a slicer that would make the pieces, so it could be mass-produced. But that's not how they did it. They made the strips on molds, as we made the perimeters, and you had to make one at a time. That's why when you order them, it takes forever to get them, and that's why they're so expensive. There were 120 prototypes, resulting in six chairs and the table. While we were developing the chairs, Knoll was sold to Westinghouse. So we were then part of Westinghouse. It was like going from an artist's studio to the army overnight.

I want to do furniture again, but it's expensive, and most companies won't spend the money. I work a lot like Eames did. I develop prototypes and somebody has to pay for that.

opposite:
pillow form studies for
bentwood chairs, 1989

[14] The chair names are derived from moves in ice hockey, Gehry's favorite game.

121

bentwood furniture 1989–1992

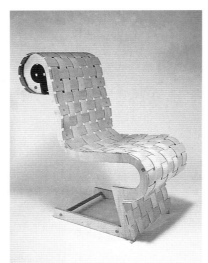

122

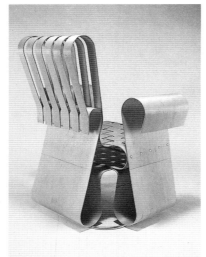

design process form created to test various ways to bend wood

123

opposite:
inspired by the lightness and flexibility of the humble bushel basket, prototypes for the bentwood chairs were developed over a two and one-half year period, 1989–1992

chairs illustated in color are in production: *Power Play with Offside*, *Cross Check*, *Hat Trick*, and *High Sticking*

bentwood funiture

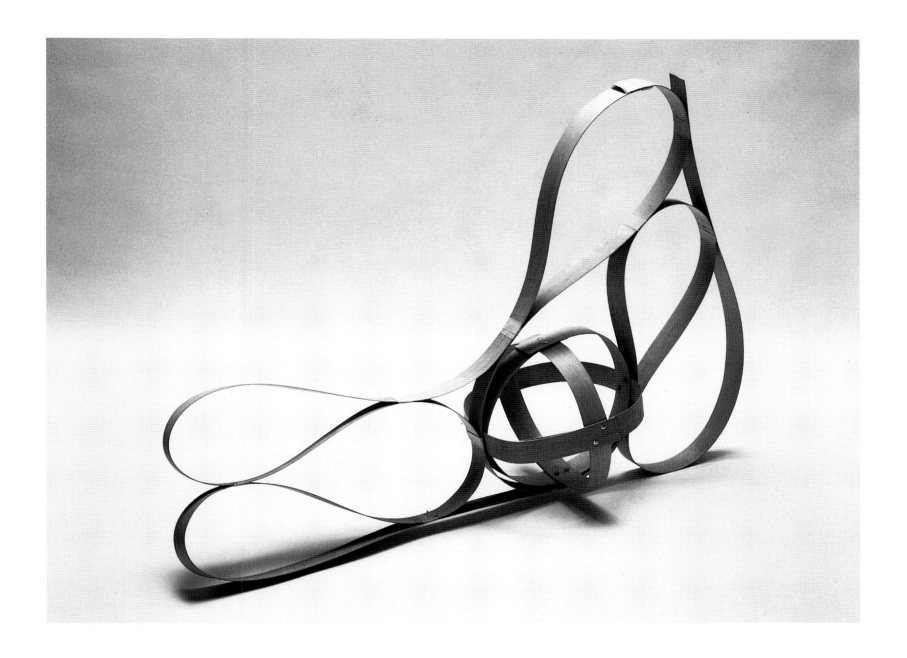

experimental chair form, 1989

opposite:
prototype chairs in the
Gehry workshop, 1990

client: Knoll   **project team:** Tom MacMichael, Daniel Sachs

project principal: Frank O. Gehry, principal/design

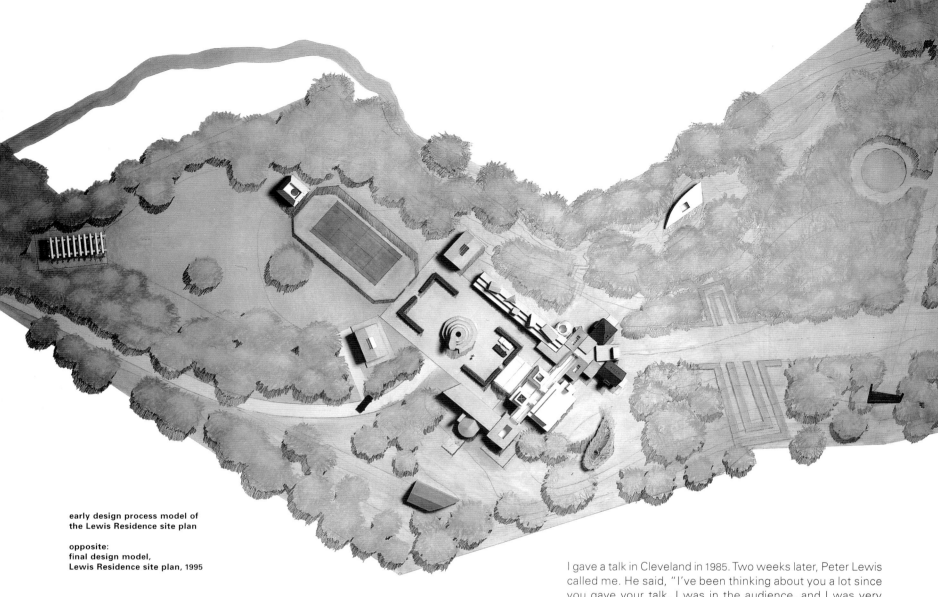

early design process model of
the Lewis Residence site plan

opposite:
final design model,
Lewis Residence site plan, 1995

lewis residence 1985–1995
(unrealized)

Lyndhurst, Ohio

I gave a talk in Cleveland in 1985. Two weeks later, Peter Lewis called me. He said, "I've been thinking about you a lot since you gave your talk. I was in the audience, and I was very moved by it. I bought an old house near a golf course. Would you consider remodeling it? I don't know how much I want to spend, maybe a million or two." At that time, that was a sizable amount for us and I didn't have many clients. So I flew back to Cleveland and met with him, and he showed me the house, and we wandered around it, and I stayed at his place, and he was very nice. He had an ex-wife who was at dinner that night. She was obviously the "art" one. She knew who and what I was. I said, "I'd be interested in doing it; we'll think about it, then we'll make a proposal."

I did a lot of studies for the remodeling. Peter kept adding things to the program. "Oh, I need a this" and "Oh, I need a that," and "I need a ten-car garage instead of...," and eventually the critical mass of the program overwhelmed the existing house. So less and less of it was left, and finally we said to each other, "Why are we doing this?" He made the big decision to knock it down and I made a plan for the whole thing.

I made a big fish pavilion looking over the golf course. It would have been all right. It probably would have gone somewhere like the Winton House.

Every time I would go to make a presentation, he'd have a film crew. On one of his birthdays he flew back the models, and he invited the governor of Ohio and many other guests to a big party. I had to make the presentation of his house to this party, which was bizarre! But I treated it like entertainment. We made a big theatrical model that filled the room—a huge foam model. A few days later, Peter showed the design to the golf club; they objected. I was told that to build this house would be a fight with the community, and he just didn't have an interest in doing that, so he abandoned the house.

Sometime later, Lewis asked me to design a new house. He wrote to me saying "I want to do it," and "This is the most important thing in my life, and I dream of this house." So I started just playing with it. Every time I put it down, I'd get some new ideas that I'd want to play with. The program changed every week. He would fly in for meetings every once in a while. I didn't work on it, and he realized I wasn't working on it. I didn't bill him. I just waited, and worked on other stuff. Then he'd have people call me to say that he really meant it, and he wrote letters to me, and finally, I had lunch with him one day, and I said the house was up to fifteen or twenty million dollars. I said, "Peter, this is stupid. You don't live like this. Why don't you just build a little five million dollar house." I said, "I can really get into that, and you can give the rest of the money to charity." Then he put his son Jonathan in charge, and I said, "Peter, Jonathan doesn't know..." "Oh yes, he knows how I want to live, and we're getting serious now." So Jonathan comes in, and demands a five million dollar sound system. Then he puts a five million dollar security system in. And then he needs a tunnel from his bedroom to get out to the hills in case he's attacked—rich guys do that. They have a safe room that's locked, which they can go into from their bedroom closet, where their clothes are. They go into the closet, and they lock a door, and they're in a concrete bunker, safe, with a whole separate communications system that gives them a direct line to the cops, to tell them that they're under siege. Then he needed storage for art, and he needed a curator for the art he was going to have in this little museum which is a 2,000-square-foot room. He has a curator, a director, a library. All of this started to build up. So the house has gone up to sixty or sixty-five million. That took it from 18,000 square feet to 42,000 square feet. He just kept adding guest-rooms. Peter has grandchildren, the house is too small, he needs this, he needs that, a pavilion. I had Philip Johnson in there doing a guesthouse. Frank Stella was going to do a guest thing. Richard Serra did the snake piece that's in Bilbao as the driveway.

Peter came to L.A., he had dinner with me one night, and he said, "How much is the house costing now?" I said, "It's sixty million, and going up. He said "How much does Bill Gates's house cost?" I said, "I don't know; I read fifty million in the paper." He said, "Well, we're okay, then." So then the guys and I met in the office, and we decided to add twenty million, because I thought it was ridiculous, and I thought we didn't

may 1991

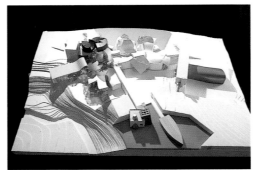

march 1992

september 1992

december 1993

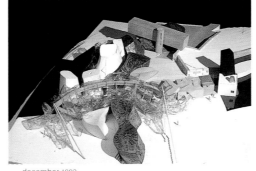

december 1993

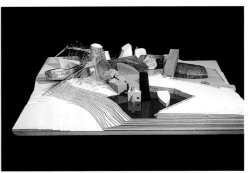

february 1994

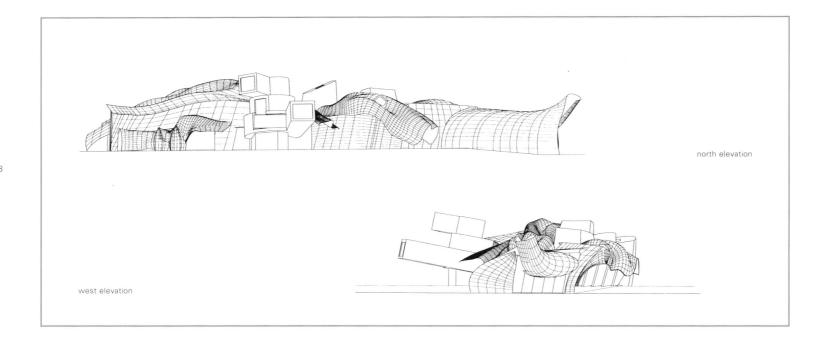

north elevation

west elevation

128

lewis residence

may 1994

november 1994

december 1994

february 1995

february 1995

final model 1995

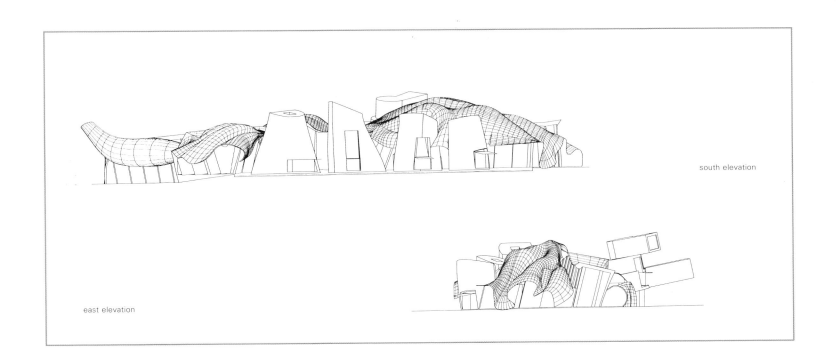

south elevation

east elevation

129

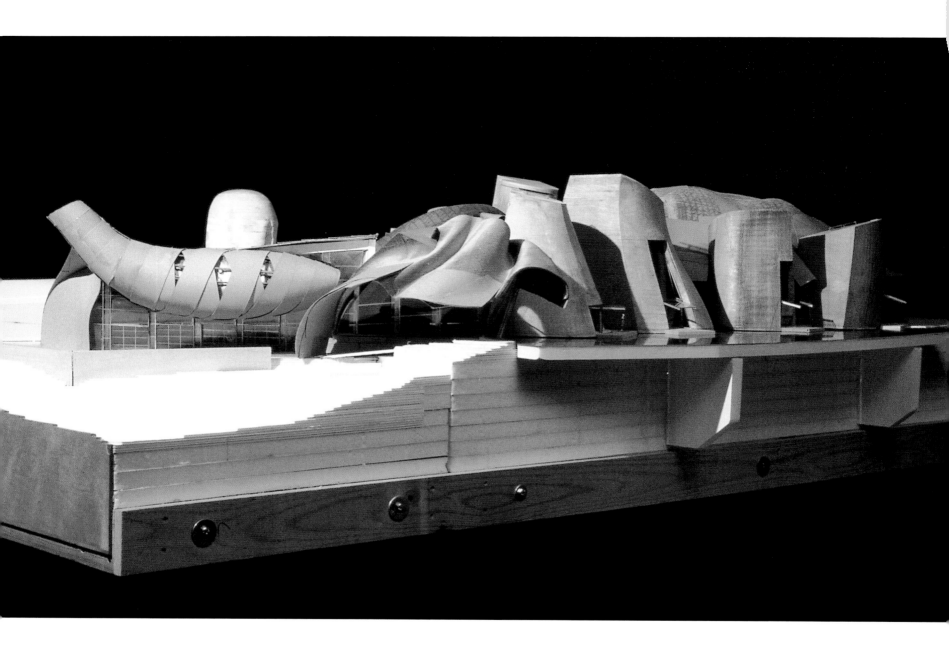

130

view from southwest of
Lewis Residence final
design model, February 1995

from left: staff rooms in fish;
kitchen in curved element;
four "sentinels": dining, living,
study, and master bedroom

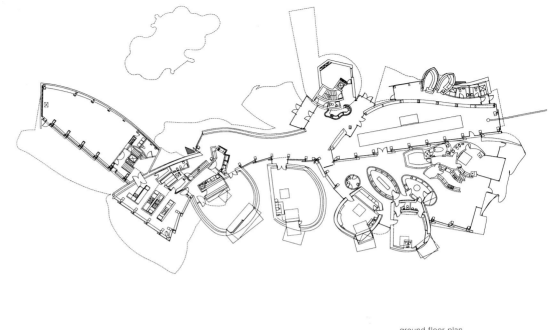

ground floor plan

upper level plan with third
and fourth circular floors above

really have costs, because we never got a chance to price it out. I was afraid of him as a client. He didn't really understand what we were doing. And you know, if you think about it, it was 42,000 square feet, one-eighth of Bilbao, and we were building Bilbao for a hundred million, and this was eighty million, so you know something was wrong. All the things Jonathan added were electronic and mechanized, and very expensive. There was six million for Oriental rugs. So Peter said, "Stop the house. I don't want any part of it." I said, "Great."

I don't know who got him back in. Anyway, a few weeks passed, he calls me back and says, "If you cut that budget in half, I'll do it." So that led to a twenty-six million dollar cost. I

wanted to conclude it, so I did it. I think in the end we would have built it for less than twenty million, but you couldn't tell him that in case we couldn't deliver. I called and told him we had it. He came over for an hour and looked at it. He said it was great, was all smiles, said, "Let's go." Then his son came to the office to work with us for three weeks. He started to list the things that weren't in the twenty-six million. He was trying to fill it back up. There were no Orientals, there were no this and that. And he told Peter we were scamming him and Peter came and we had a terrible meeting. Later Peter called me from his plane, and he said, "I have a solution for all of this. I'm going to build the Philip Johnson piece and the

design process model of conservatory with fish as bath and dressing area

opposite:
design process model; garage and fish guest room/staff quarters, November 1994

design process model; early version of sentinels, April 1994

design process model; early version of sentinels, February 1994

garage with the fish, and put the swimming pool in the garage." I said, "Peter, I wouldn't do that. But you go ahead and do it. You've got the design. Do it. I can't do that." So then he fussed around about it, and then he called me and said he'd like to have some remembrance of all this, some models, drawings. I said, "Sure. What do you want? Come out and pick it. There are models all over the place." I said, "Peter, you name the date when you want them, and I'm ready. I have the drawings and models for you." I said, "I'll make a special one; give me a couple of weeks. I'll do a small model you can hang on the wall, because I don't know where you're going to put the big stuff." And I said, "I'll pay for it;

no charge." And he was happy with that. I had a dinner party for him in L.A., and invited Tom Krens. Krens came, because by now Peter was on the Guggenheim Board and I was working there.

Then the next call came from him. He said, "I'm about to give a bunch of money to Case Western to do a business school. The president told me I could select the architect, and I select you." I said, "Are you involved with it?" He said, "No. I won't be involved. I'm just giving money."

I have alleged that the Lewis house was the most important thing in my life, and that it gave me the equivalent of a MacArthur Grant, and ideas for Bilbao.

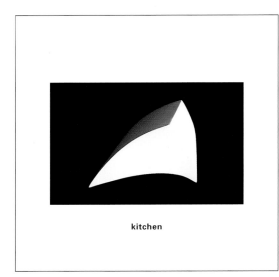

kitchen

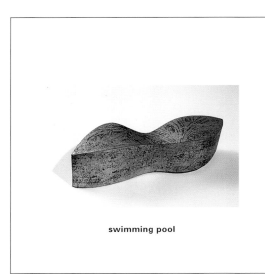

swimming pool

dressing room and bathroom

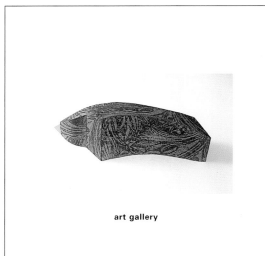

art gallery

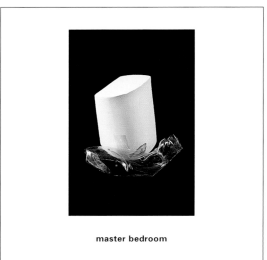

master bedroom

atrium

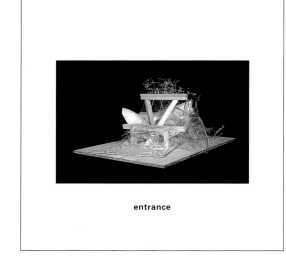

entrance

guest house (Philip Johnson)

garage

opposite: dining room with glass fish porch

134

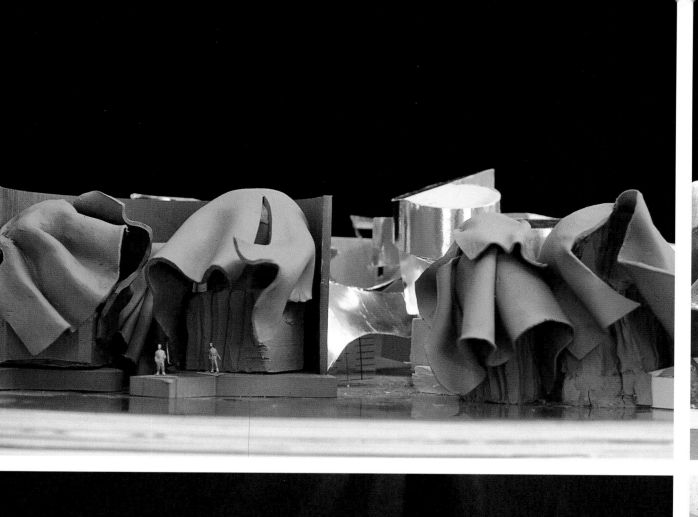

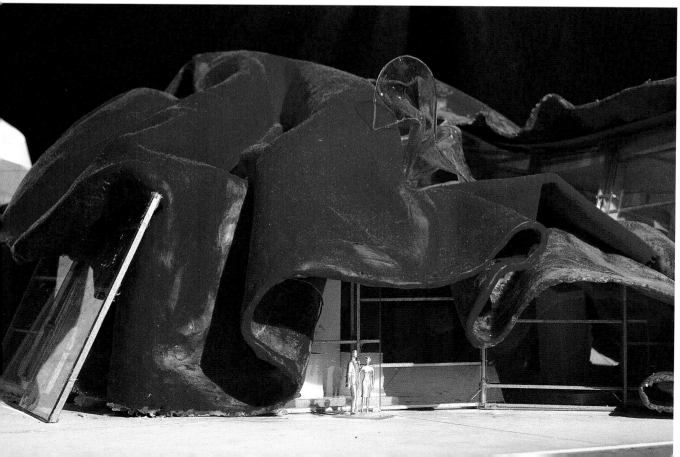

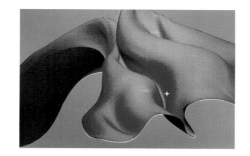

three examples of Catia three-dimensional documentation of conservatory exterior skin

final design model of horse's head entry hall and gallery, 1995

opposite:
design process clay model; early version of sentinels, October 1993

design process waxed felt model of conservatory at pool, February 1995

design process waxed felt model of conservatory, February 1995

conservatory roof; final design model of computer-milled layers of paper and resin, February 1995

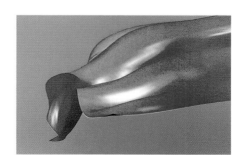

The unrealized Lewis residence was a fascinating ten-year saga involving an idiosyncratic client who challenged the world's most daring architect to create the world's most astonishing house. Its final 22,000-square-foot design included a kitchen, dining room, living room, entry hall, two master bedrooms, a study, a conservatory, and an enclosed lap pool. Philip Johnson designed one guest house. In addition there were staff quarters and a five-car garage. The house was to be located on a nine-acre wooded site that included a complex landscape design and outdoor sculptures. This project provided Gehry with an opportunity to pursue ideas close to pure form, in a way rarely available to architects. In its various incarnations the seeds of projects undertaken simultaneously and of several to come can be found in the long series of drawings and models that record the evolution of this most unusual, exuberant project.

design process model of a sentinel

opposite:
final design model; view from northeast with pool (left), sauna, and steam bath; guest house (middle); and guest house (right) by Philip Johnson, February 1995

client: Peter B. Lewis

project pricipals: Frank O. Gehry, design principal
James Glymph, project principal
Craig Webb, Susan Desko, Vince Snyder, project designers
Terry Bell, George Metzger, Laurence Tighe, project architects

project team: Rich Barrett, Karl Blette, Naomi Ehrenpreis,
John Goldsmith, Michael Jobes, Michael Mantzoris,
Jay Park, David Redy, Philip Rowe, Eva Sobesky, Kevin
Sutherland, Tensho Takemori, Robert Thibodeau, Lisa
Towning, Dane Twichell, Scott Uriu, Jeff Wauer, Kristin
Woehl, Nora Wolin, Brian Yoo

collaborating architect: Philip Johnson Architects

artists: Richard Serra, Larry Bell, Maggie Cheswick-Jencks

The Center for the Visual Arts was part of the Toledo Museum of Art, which has three large porches with Greek-style pediments. It's a beautiful white marble building. The Center was in the basement. There were several choices for the site. You could put a separate building outside, across the road, or somewhere else. After spending time with the people, I realized the value of the students being in the same building with the art. It's a great art department. I thought if the Center is separated, the kids will go to their cars and leave, and they'll never go in the museum. They'll always say, "Well, some day I'll go in there." So I argued that it had to be connected, and prevailed.

We decided to connect with a student art gallery that would take you into the bottom. The theater is in there at the lower level, and there is a foyer where they have art shows, and so we thought they should have people come through the student gallery that could also be the entrance. I made this very compact.

You couldn't add a white marble piece; it would destroy the existing building, and anyway, we couldn't afford marble. So we used lead-coated copper, and we made three kinds of shapes, very tightly compacted. The marble building is in the trees, and in front of it is a Marc di Suvero sculpture. The new building looks like another sculpture beside it—a big one.

The new art school has a linear L-shape that creates a courtyard adjacent to the existing Toledo Museum of Art building. It is physically connected to the museum through a student art gallery. The three-story building has an iridescent lead-coated copper skin and green-tinted windows that contrast with the white marble of the Beaux-Arts museum, and relate to the green patina of its copper roof. Skylights bring natural light to the studios and classrooms on the upper floors. Lecture halls and photography studios are in the basement. Two glass-enclosed stair towers form the ends of the glass-enclosed corridor surrounding the courtyard.

university of toledo center
for the visual arts 1990–1992

Toledo, Ohio

third level plan

lobby
office
drawing
lounge
painting

second level plan

lobby
office
design/foundations
print making

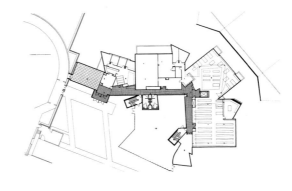

ground level plan

entry
student gallery
conference
administration
library
art supply
lobby
sculpture court

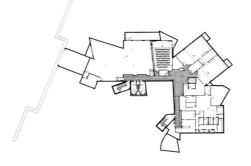

basement level plan

lobby
mechanical room
art history lecture
art education
photography

toledo center for the visual arts

146

east elevation (and north
elevation, opposite)
with sunlight reflecting on
lead-coated copper cladding

previous page:
view from the north of glass wall
surrounding open courtyard

client: The Toledo Museum of Art

project principals: Frank O. Gehry, design principal
James Glymph, David Denton, project principals
Peter Locke, Randall Stout, project architects
C. Gregory Walsh, Michael Maltzan, project designers

project team: Andres Alper,
Jon Drezner, Michael Resnic,
Tami Wedekind

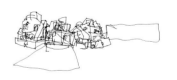

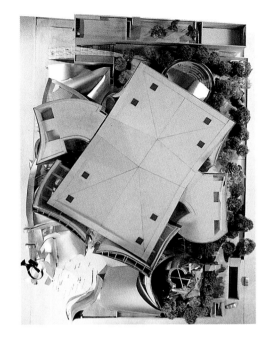

aerial view, final design model

opposite:
detail of final design model
showing main entrance at
Grand Avenue and 1st Street.

walt **disney concert hall** 1987–
Los Angeles, California

People say the Concertgebouw in Amsterdam is the best hall for music. Well, if you sit in the back, it is. If you sit under the balcony, it isn't. If you sit behind the orchestra, where 700 people sit, it's a different experience. But it has the cachet of years of great conductors making recordings there. Boston Symphony Hall is a shoebox. If you sit in the front twelve rows in the orchestra, you can't hear a thing. The only place you hear well is up in the balcony in the cheap seats, because there's enough reverb time. It is the best in certain places. So what I'm saying is, the beauty is in the ear of the beholder. It varies and a lot depends on the conductor. The musical result is affected if the orchestra is good that day. If the orchestra is balanced, if the brass section isn't too loud because you have a bunch of high-powered trumpeters whose lungs need to be exercised, if there's a particularly inspired bass section in the music and there's a bass response to the whole—there are all kinds of factors.

Ernest Fleischmann [former Executive Director of the Los Angeles Philharmonic Association] said, "I want the Berlin Philharmonic; that's what I want." If you follow the acoustics, there are some similarities that the acoustical criteria create. The seating is prescribed, because there's a certain size for the orchestra, and there are fixed sight lines. If you decide to make a surround hall, then you end up with a hall that's very close to Berlin. Surround hall means you have audience in front, on the side, and behind. A surround hall allows you to make the room 110 feet instead of 70 feet long. Then the acoustical requirements make you do this kind of stuff on the top, off to the side, so that the sound reflects. You get a lot of similarities by following the rules of the game. It's not that I copied Hans Scharoun. It's that the game was the same, and the client asked for the same diagram.

I can show you a lot of halls that I didn't do. One that Kevin Roche did, and I've seen halls that Hugh Hardy has done, and I've seen halls that others have done, and mine looks as though it's in the gene pool. But the genes do not define stylistic relationships as much as acoustical relationships. They create similarities. It's kind of inevitable. If you follow the same criteria, you end up with a similar language and the halls start to look alike.

Ernest used to talk about the Scharoun building, and I'd seen pictures of it but I'd never been in it. Before I won the competition I went to Berlin on my own, and I went to the Scharoun building where I met Scharoun's assistant. I had dinner with him, and we talked a lot about what he did. He built the chamber hall after the concert hall was completed. So I went to a concert in the Scharoun building and then I went to a concert in the chamber hall, and I realized that the chamber hall didn't work. The magic that Scharoun had didn't translate. I think it's in your fingertips. It's not a conscious thing. I think you create that intuitively. It has to do with yourself and your people. And Scharoun had that. It's a wonderful place to be because the place puts people together and makes it easy. It's hard to be alone in Berlin. I went to five concerts alone in Berlin, and every time I went to a concert, I met people. If you were a single woman and went to a concert in Berlin, you wouldn't feel awkward meeting people. I felt very comfortable

competition model

a long series of design process models (left and opposite) was made for the building when it was designed to be clad in stone. Those have been succeeded by recent studies of the building clad in metal, 1987–

opposite:
design process model, stone, looking at main entrance at Grand Avenue and 1st Street

design process model, stone and metal, looking at the corner of Grand Avenue and 2nd Street

final design model, metal, Grand Avenue elevation

being alone. I understood what it was like. I went to the bar, I had a drink, I went to the bookstore, I ran into people. You bumped into people. And when you went into the hall it was like that, and it made the connection to the orchestra, and I never left that place without having met someone, had a drink with them—interesting people—and felt welcome. So then you go to the library by Scharoun, and it's exactly the same. People sitting around, kids sitting around, and it's easy to meet people. You walk in as a stranger; the building allows and engenders and encourages, in some miraculous way, a kind of interaction.

Originally Disney Hall was to be stone. Then the client saw the American Center, which wasn't sealed and not maintained, and the stone got dirty, so everybody was worried about it. They thought I didn't know what I was doing. They were all out to get me here because I'm the local guy, and they think I'm "chain-linking." So they started a barrage coming at me. Finally I said, "I don't care if it's toothpicks. If you really want me to look at it in metal, I'll do it." So I just took two weeks off, and designed it in metal, and they all love it now. It saved ten million dollars, so they're all happy, and I like it better.

We went with the shiny finish for the Weisman Museum because of the light in Minneapolis. It finally dawned on me

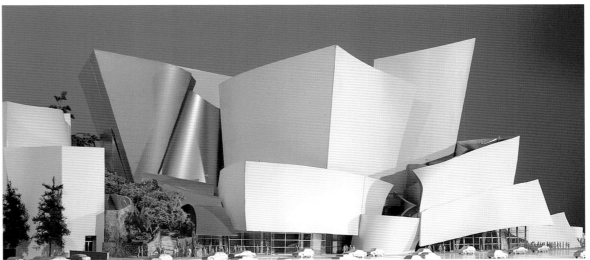

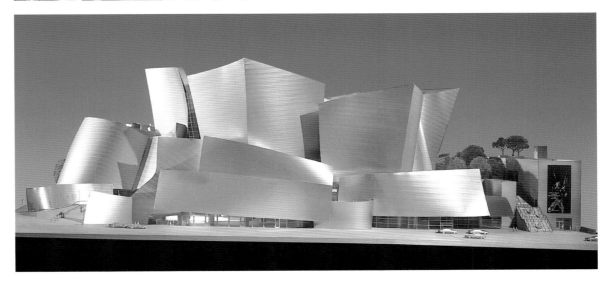

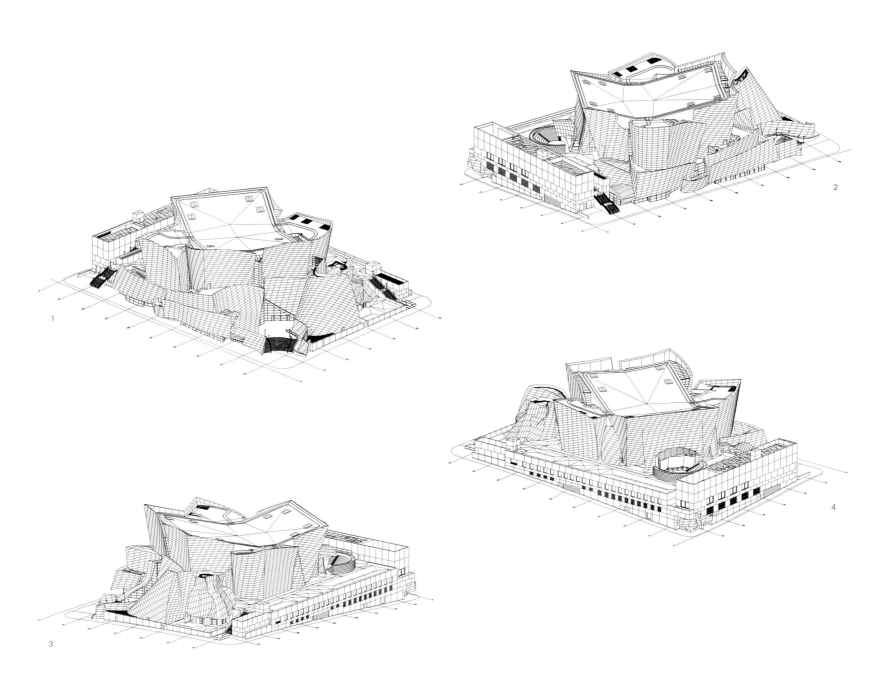

152

1 axonometric looking southwest   2 axonometric looking northwest   3 axonometric looking northeast   4 axonometric looking southeast

walt disney concert hall

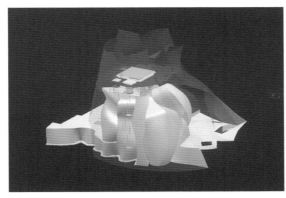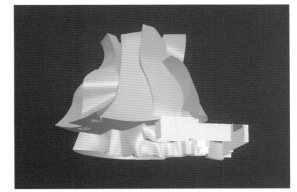

Catia shaded surface models:

the exterior of the Founders' Room (upper right)

the Founders' Room with the exterior wall transparent and the shell of the interior wall visible (upper left)

the Founders' Room ceiling, looking up (middle)

model showing isolated ceiling section (bottom left)

close up view of the Founders' Room ceiling (bottom right)

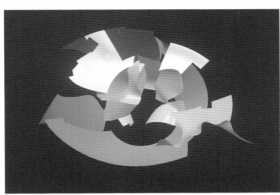

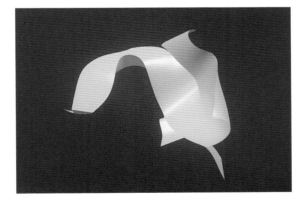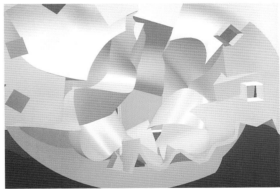

that that wasn't going to work. We couldn't use it in L.A. It would look like a big refrigerator. At Bard College and in L.A. titanium won't work because they don't do the same thing as Bilbao with the light. In Bilbao on a gray day the titanium turns golden. But it doesn't here. Except for El Niño, it doesn't rain here often. Mostly you get sunny days, and the stainless steel that we're thinking of becomes white in the sun, so we're going to explore that.

The reason metal is nice is that it will be a very big contrast with the existing hall and with the museum across the street. I'm happy with it. It also allowed me to refine some of the forms and play with them. It made it more exciting because

now it's a new project. In the old scheme, it always looked like the building hit Grand Avenue and got flattened slightly, and I could never make it three-dimensional. When I flipped those, it worked somehow. I don't know why. So that's why we're changing it. I want to use white marble. There's the stainless and the white. We're not going to make the metal like Bilbao. It's going to be thick, so it's not going to pillow. It's going to be smooth. There are going to be cut joints. Tight, like airplanes.

walt disney concert hall

large-scale design process model
with modelmaker at work

variations on the concert hall
interior in a series of thirty design
process models

opposite:
final design model of concert
hall interior

overleaf:
final design model of pipe organ

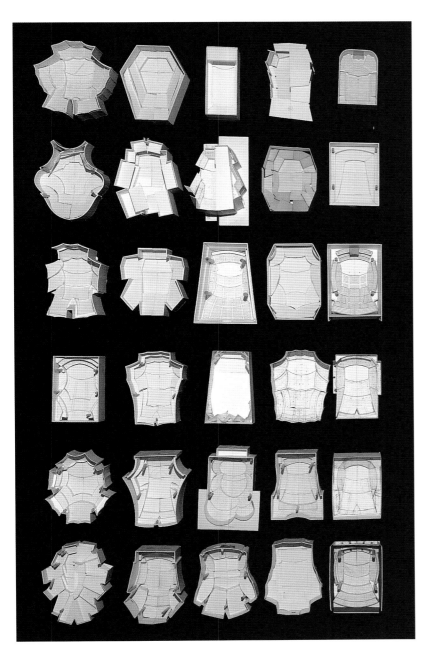

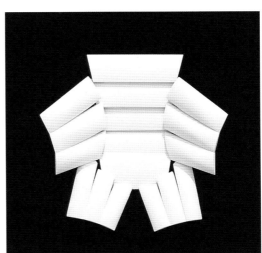

This most controversial of all Gehry projects, the Walt Disney Concert
Hall will at last go forward, to become the permanent home of the
Los Angeles Philharmonic Orchestra. Located on Bunker Hill adjacent to the Dorothy Chandler Music Pavilion and across Grand Avenue from the Museum of Contemporary Art, this important addition
to the city's cultural life will bring renewed vitality to this historically
significant neighborhood.

The 2,293-seat hall is lined with wood seating blocks and sail-like
ceiling elements. A huge pipe organ will fill the rear stage. The hall
will have natural light via skylights and a large window opposite the
stage. An underground parking lot for 2,500 cars is already in place.
Much of the site is devoted to gardens that will be accessible from all
areas of the building.

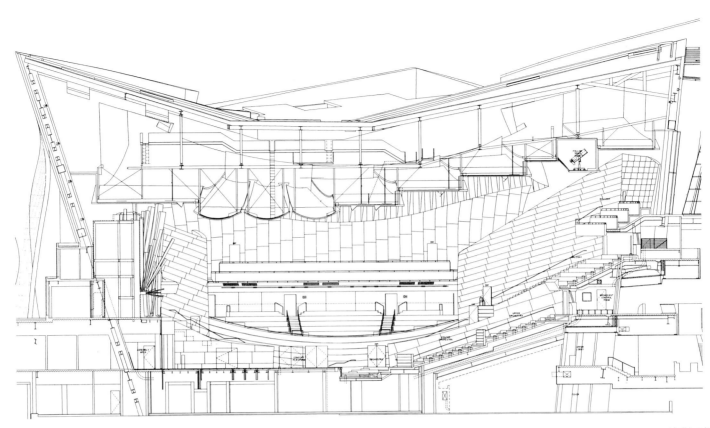

concert hall longitudinal section

concert hall axonometric looking south

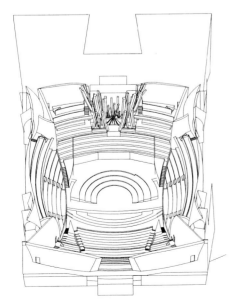

concert hall reflected ceiling plan

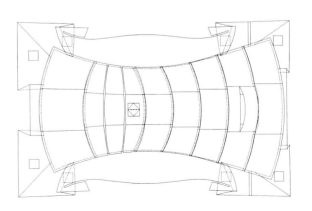

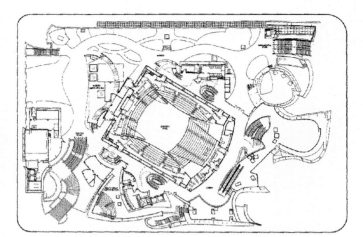

floor plan, balcony level

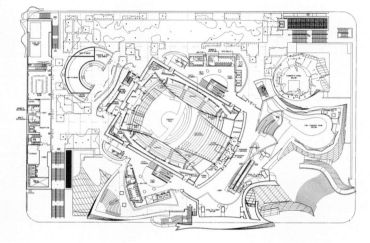

floor plan, main level

158

**design process model of
the Founders' Room
ceiling, and (opposite)
various interior spaces**

walt disney concert hall

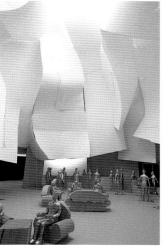

159

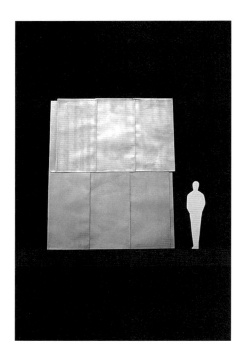

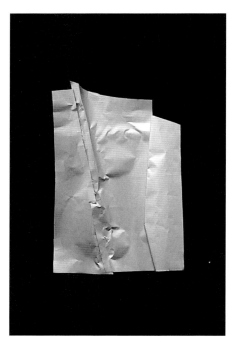

walt disney concert hall

design process model of a fountain,
dedicated to Lillian B. Disney,
the wife of Walt Disney, who was
the instigator and primary funder
of the Disney Hall project

opposite:
studies for exterior metal cladding

overleaf:
final design model from
1st Street and Hope Street
showing Founders' Room
and gardens

client: Walt Disney Concert Hall Committee

project principals: Frank O. Gehry, design principal
James Glymph, project principal
Vano Haritunians, project manager
Craig Webb and Michael Maltzan, project designers
Terry Bell and Craig Webb, project architects

Catia modeling: Nick Easton, Gary Lundberg,
Bruce Shepard, Rick Smith, Kristen Woehl

project team: Andrew Alper, Suren Ambartsumyan, Larik Ararat, Kamran Ardalan, Herwig Baumgartner, Pejman Berjis, Rick Black, Kirk Blaschke, Tomaso Bradshaw, Earle Briggs, John Carter, Padraic Cassidy, William Childers, Rebeca Cotera, Jonathan Davis, Jim Dayton, Denise Disney, Jon Drezner, Jeff Guga, David Hardie, James Jackson, Victoria Jenkins, Michael Jobes, Michael Kempf, Gregory Kromhout, Naomi Langer, Jacquine Lorange, Gerhard Mayer, Alex Meconi, Emilio Melgazo, George Metzger, Brent Miller, Julianna Morais, Rosemary Morris, Mathias Mortenson, Gaston Nogues, David Pakshong, Michael Resnic, David Rodriguez, Christopher Samuelian, Michael J. Sant, Robert Seelenbacher, Michael Sedlacek, Matthias Seufert, Tadao Shimizu, Eva Sobesky, Randall Stout, Thomas Swanson, John Sziachta, Tensho Takemori, Larry Tighe, Hiroshi Tokumaru, Jose Catriel Tulian, Dane Twichell, William Ullman, Monica Valtierra-Day, Yu-Wen Wang, Eric Wegerbauer, Gretchen Werner, Adam Wheeler, Tim Williams, Brian Yoo, Brian Zamora

walt disney concert hall

164

the Washington Avenue bridge
crosses the Mississippi River at
the Weisman Museum on
the University of Minnesota's
west bank

opposite:
detail of west façade

By the time of the Weisman Museum, we could no longer use lead copper outside, so I went to stainless. I'd seen a number of Ellsworth Kelly's sandblasted stainless sculptures, and I loved them because they looked like suede. I was going to use it on the Weisman. We made mockups, and put them on the site. And then the worst thing happened: when they put the salt on the road for the snow, it pocked the surface, and the metal developed rust spots. So the university said, "You can't use it because of the rust spots." I was devastated.

A few days later I was taking my son Sami to hockey camp, and we went to see the sandblasted mockup; it was raining and the metal looked dull—it just looked dead. I had had a shiny stainless mockup made also, but I was worried about it because I thought, you can't do a shiny stainless-steel building. A week later, I went back to pick up Sami and we stayed all day in Minneapolis to look at the site and at the shiny stainless sample. It was one of those days that went gray and sunny. Sami said to me, "Papa, you've got to go for it." I just needed that little push. I knew that what he was saying was right. I'll never forget, he said, "Papa, go for it."

To develop the lighting scheme we built a mockup at the Santa Monica Airport and we worked with PHA Lighting Design; they make custom fixtures. This is the way you do it. You've got to get to the fixture people. At the Weisman we made a shelf, and we projected light up on the ceiling to get ambient light, and then we had track lighting in addition. When the Weisman was built, they didn't use the fixture that we had designed. They bought another off-the-shelf fixture. When their fixture is lighted, it makes the panel above brighter than the panel below. It destroys the wall, because you look at the bright panel, so they just turn it off.

Critics of the building say that it turns its back on the campus's central mall. It now embraces the bridge and beckons to the east campus. But we designed it so that it has two faces, and they just left the second one out. This will be corrected when the addition they've asked us to think about is appended to the east side of the building.

frederick r. **weisman** museum 1990–1993
Minneapolis, Minnesota

The Weisman Art Museum plays two roles. In addition to giving the University of Minnesota its long-awaited art museum, it adorns the Mississippi River with the extraordinary shining sculpture of its west façade, which responds to the setting sun and the flowing water below with fascinating reflections and ever-changing forms. The museum, perched on the western edge of the campus, is distributed on four levels. The beautifully scaled galleries, bathed in controlled natural light from sculptural skylights, are on the third, main level. The offices are on the fourth, taking advantage of the city views. Connected to the city by a bridge that ends at its main entrance, pedestrians coming off the bridge are literally drawn into the building beneath its stainless-steel canopy supported by Gehry's signature tree-trunklike legs. The other museum façades are brick, as are the majority of buildings on the east and west campuses.

168

longitudinal section through the galleries

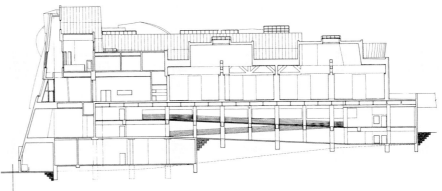

client: University of Minnesota Art and Teaching Museum

project principals: Frank O. Gehry, design principal
Robert Hale, project principal
Victoria Jenkins, Matt Fineout, project architects
Edwin Chan, project designer

project team: David Gastrau,
Richard Rosa

**night view with installation of
Gehry fish lamp**

**opposite:
view of stainless-steel cladding
on west façade**

frederick r. weisman museum

site plan

That's how I started—doing social housing—when I was a kid. There are lots of social housing projects in my portfolio. They are projects that were never built.

I don't believe there is a chance to create credible social housing in America at this time. We used to have FHA, and I did a lot of work on FHA projects when I was young.[15] I always felt a responsibility; I felt that we should all be trying to do that kind of housing, and that you could bring good architecture to that kind of housing. That was a fantasy that few people shared. FHA's bureaucracy overlays were designed to eliminate architecture. Today there's no real social housing legislation in America. There hasn't been the kind of drive necessary to make it happen. In Germany there is, although it's not perfect there.

Germany has created a public corporation that has its own profit center. It has to meet criteria as though it's a private business, and it's empowered to make deals in acquiring land, hiring architects, and building social housing. They have many sites around Frankfurt. We were invited to workshops in Frankfurt to create competitive schemes for social housing. Six architects were brought together for three days, given a

goldstein **sud housing** 1991–1996
Frankfurt, Germany

site, and each was asked to do a scheme and present it. At the end of that exercise the corporation would choose the scheme to be built. I won a competition to do a thousand units of housing in Frankfurt. It's a project called Bon Amis. It's still on the books. We're still supposed to do it, but they're not doing it yet. Because we'd won that rather large competition, they gave us Goldstein, a smaller one, in the meantime.

They are very sophisticated and they are very art-wise. We had to stick to a budget. The housing is completely subsidized. We were there for the opening. People had already moved in, and we had a big party. I met with all the people, and paraded through the town. They seemed happy. I should go back.

[15] The FHA (Federal Housing Administration) was established in 1934. It was an agency that provided long-term loans at low interest rates in order to encourage and stabilize home ownership in the United States. In 1965 it became part of HUD (Housing and Urban Development).

final design site model

opposite:
zinc-clad housing unit

Goldstein Sud includes 162 housing units, a parking area, a social center, and small neighboorood shops. It is located between a green-belt and a public park, and is the last housing to be built in an area that includes a number of social housing developments. Floor plans vary according to their relationship to the site's amenities—schools, sports facilities, etc.—and to solar orientation. The units are from three to five stories in U-shaped configurations. Stucco walls are painted in vivid warm colors, and the trapezoidal balconies, entry canopies, stair towers, and other small buildings are zinc clad.

client: Nassauische Heimstatte

project principals: Frank O. Gehry, design principal
Jim Glymph, project principal
Randall Stout, project designer/architect
Michael Maltzan, project designer
Tomaso Bradshaw, job captain

project team: Jonathan Davis,
David Denton, Mara Dworsky,
Robert Hale, Michael Resnic,
Matthias Seufert, Eva Sobesky,
Hiroshi Tokumaru, Tim Williams

We've designed a number of gateway buildings: Weisman, Prague, Iowa, and more. But it's not by intent; it's coincidence. Even the Seattle project has the monorail going through it, just as the bridge goes into Bilbao.

Tom Krens talked about the Wright atrium a lot.[16] I realized Frank Lloyd Wright wasn't interested in the kind of art I'm interested in, and he ignored it. So he created a building that was antithetical to the art. I said to Krens, I don't think the building has to be that antagonistic to the art. But he thought the atrium should be a contentious piece, and should provoke artists. So that's what I picked up on. If you look at the first iterations, it's boxy and square, like a quarry, and I saw the walls as shelves where you could hang the work. Tom said, "Do something else. Take it on. Make it better than Wright. Make a great space, and we'll deal with it, and then let's review it."

There are gestures in my sketches. How do you get them built? I was able to build them with the computer, with material I would never have tried before. You'll see the relationship to my sketches in Bilbao. This is the first time I've gotten it. And once you taste blood, you're not going to give up. I don't know where it can go. How wiggly can you get and still make a building?

I used to be a symmetrical freak and a grid freak. I used to follow grids and then I started to think and I realized that those were chains, that Frank Lloyd Wright was chained to the 30-60 grid, and there was no freedom in it for him, and that grids are an obsession, a crutch. You don't need that if you can create spaces and forms and shapes. That's what artists do, and they don't have grids and crutches, they just do it.

The Winton house plan is a kind of pinwheel form. It came into focus again on the Lewis house, when I started plunking down forms, and then I realized that the plan of the Lewis house was very unusual. When you drew the plan, it was weird. I had never seen anything like it. Then I carried those ideas into Bilbao, and when I drew the plan of Bilbao I was so happy, because I realized that it was a beautiful thing. I'd never seen anything like it except in those buildings. It just evolved. I didn't consciously do it, but it intuitively evolved.

It's a very long way from one room, what I used to call the "white canvas," to Bilbao. I enjoy the complexity of a big project, trying to organize it. It's different from one room, but I think the one-room idea gave me the beginning of a way to

guggenheim museum bilbao 1991–1997
Bilbao, Spain

randy jefferson: In Bilbao we set up a series of rules, but the rules weren't derived because of limitations of the computer; they were derived to control costs. Going into the project, we knew that we had an extremely tough budget. It's easy for a budget to slip from $300 to $400 a square foot. So we began Bilbao with some very important ground rules as to how we were going to develop the complex shapes and maintain control of the budget.

The titanium surface on Bilbao is about 0.38 millimeters. It's not a whole lot thicker than several pieces of paper. Each sheet is approximately two feet by three feet and the joint is a traditional locked seam that has been used with copper for decades. What's beautiful about it—on a very windy day you actually see the titanium sheets flutter. The pressure across the surface creates alternating positive and negative pressures. The wind pressure pushes and pulls on the surface. You can see a pillowing that is a product of the thinness of the metal and the system of connecting it to the wall construction. The edges are very stiff because of the locked seam, and there's a clip that sits in the fold to hold the titanium on the wall.

[16] This reference is to the atrium of Frank Lloyd Wright's Solomon R. Guggenheim Museum building on Fifth Avenue in Manhattan.

descending steps lead to the museum's main entrance

opposite:
view of the museum seen from surrounding hillside

break down the scale of big things. Scale is a struggle. How do you make a big monolithic building that's humane? I try to fit into the city. In Bilbao I took on the bridge, the river, the road, and then tried to make a building that was scaled to the nineteenth-century city.

Then I said to myself, "Artists have trouble with scale in the city because the city is such a large scale. No one ever commissions artists to make sixty-story sculptures, and until one of them makes a sixty-story sculpture, their works will not stand beside the Empire State Building and mean anything." I thought, if you could metaphorically create a city that would allow them to play, that might work. Then I realized that this was an opportunity to make something in the tradition of the great metaphorical cities. And that's what led to what's there, using the ramps and the stairs as a kind of metaphorical city—a metropolis.

One thing is certain: artists want to be in an important place. Go back to my Walker [Art Center] show, when it came to MOCA [Museum of Contemporary Art, Los Angeles]. I said "Put it in the TC" [Temporary Contemporary], and you said "No way." And you were right. If I'd gone to the TC, the building would have marginalized me. Not only that, but it was the contrast between Isozaki and me that was interesting. The artists are very positive about Bilbao. I've gotten a lot of letters. It was Tom Krens's idea to have galleries for living artists different from galleries for dead artists. In the end it was a pretty good strategy.

Lighting is always a difficult, complex problem. So in Bilbao we said, "Okay, we'll put the lights in and never move them." We wanted to wash the walls with light, so we put the fixtures every twelve feet, and they are never changed.

I love to go back to Bilbao. They're all part of my family now.

design process model (1992–1993)

final design model (1994)

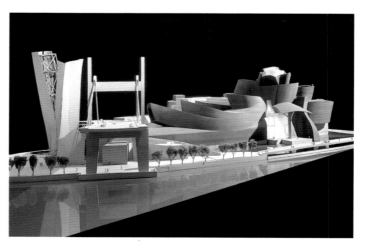

final design model (1994)

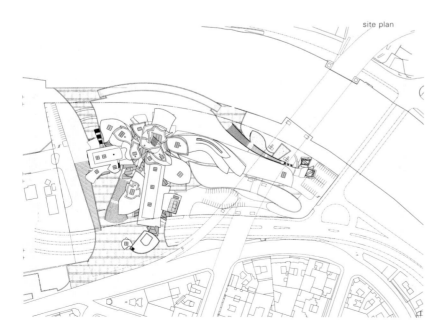

site plan

guggenheim museum bilbao

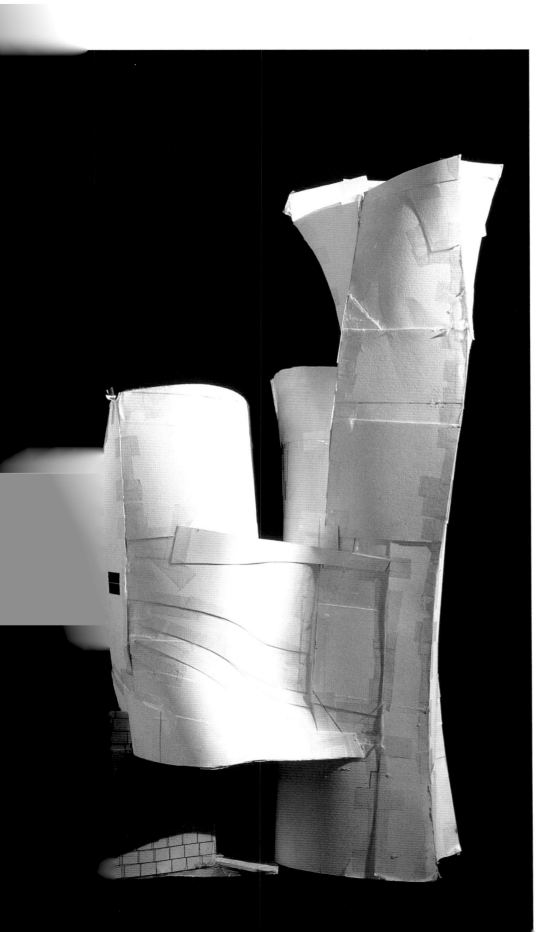

design process model (1992–1993)

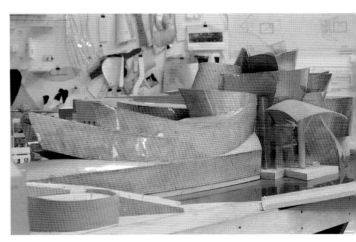

final design model (1994)

design process model (1992–1993)

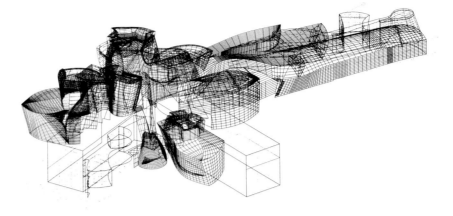

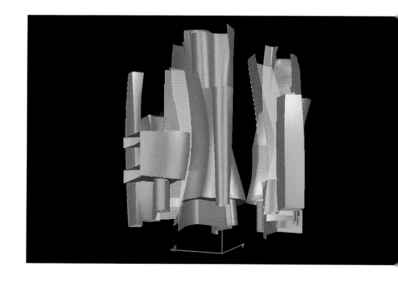

atrium

this page and opposite:
axonometric drawings

Catia studies of atrium and tower

guggenheim museum bilbao

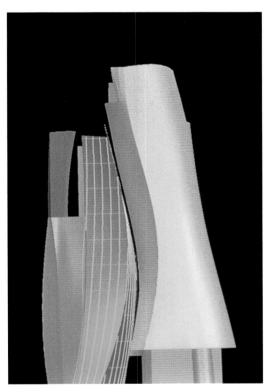

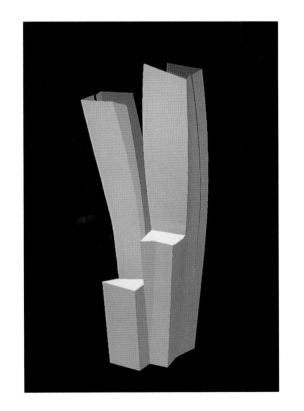

view of north elevation, water garden, and walkway over the Nervión River

guggenheim museum bilbao

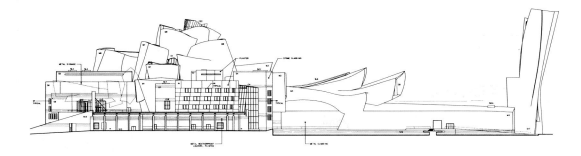

south elevation

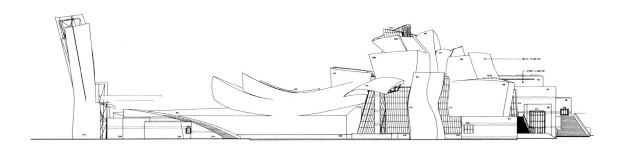

north elevation

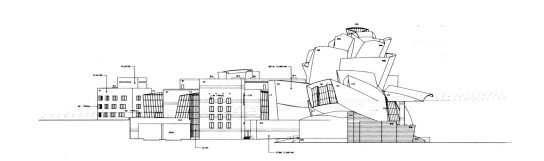

east elevation

183

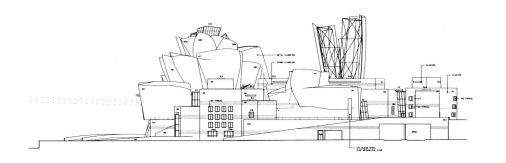

west elevation

184

guggenheim museum bilbao

186

partial view of north elevation

opposite:
partial view of east elevation

page 184: two views of the
titanium cladding

page 185: steel framework
under construction

A collaboration between the Basque Country Administration, which owns and funds the project, and the Solomon R. Guggenheim Foundation, which operates the museum and provides the basic art collection, the museum is part of an ambitious redevelopment plan for this area of the Nervión River. The 297,000-square-foot museum incorporates an existing bridge that connects the nineteenth-century city to outlying districts. The central atrium rises 164 feet above the river and is flooded with light through its sculptural skylights. The exterior rectangular building elements are covered in limestone; the curvilinear forms are sheathed in titanium. The office area exterior is vivid blue stucco. The galleries correspond to the directions of the exterior: rectilinear spaces house traditional modernist works from the Guggenheim collection, while the asymmetrical galleries with curving walls are devoted to commissioned works and temporary exhibitions.

installation in process of works by
Richard Serra for a 1999 exhibition

bottom and opposite:
the gallery installed for the
museum's opening in 1998,
including works by Robert Morris,
Lawrence Weiner, Richard Serra,
and Claes Oldenburg

190

partial view of atrium skylights

opposite:
view from above of
164-foot-tall atrium

night view of north elevation

client: Solomon R. Guggenheim Foundation
Consorcio Del Proyecto Guggenheim Bilbao

project principals: Frank O. Gehry, design principal
Randy Jefferson, project principal
Vano Haritunians, project manager
Douglas Hanson, project architect
Edwin Chan, project designer

project team: Rich Barrett, Karl Blette, Tomaso Bradshaw, Matt Fineout, Robert Hale, Dave Hardie, Michael Hootman, Grzegorz Kosmal, Naomi Langer, Mehran Mashayekh, Chris Mercier, Brent Miller, David Reddy, Marc Salette, Bruce Shepard, Rick Smith, Eva Sobesky, Derek Soltes, Todd Spiegel, Jeff Wauer, Kristin Woehl

guggenheim museum bilbao

roof plan

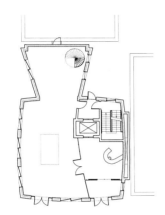

ground level plan

üstra office building 1995–
Hannover, Germany

The nine-story, 21,000-square-foot office building for Üstra Hannover Public Transportation is one of a series of new towers to be constructed in a historic district adjacent to open parkland. Peter Ruthenburg, who ran the bus stop program, was hired to do other projects, including this office building. [Gehry was one of ten architects invited to create a bus stop for Hannover, as a prologue to the city's Expo 2000.] The bus company has a tiny corner lot next to a square; it's close to a main tram stop.

They started with a straight low-rise box. Ruthenburg wondered if we could do something with it. Everything I did looked very complicated and contrived. I looked at the relationship of the site to the square and I realized that this site was really important. So then I started playing with it, and finally twisted it, and that was that. As the building rises it twists in the direction of the open park area. The exterior is stainless steel. We're looking at a scratchy surface finish. The only problem I have with the scratchy stuff is that it gets close to David Smith, and I don't want to trivialize what he did. And also, it's a little bit glitzy when the light hits it. It's the kind of building where the simpler it is the better.

In Germany all the windows in high-rise buildings must open. That's why you see all these double facades now: glass on the outside and the inside. In the Hannover building the interior window opens by sliding it into a wall pocket. We did it in Prague too. There's a draft in between the two layers that lets air in. They have a system in which they can leave the draft open, or closed. If it gets cold, they can take the hot air in with little fans that take the air in and out. The people generate more heat than the building needs. In the winter they need heat only in the morning and at night.

By law, German buildings aren't air-conditioned. The hotels may have air conditioning, but not the office buildings. Most American high-rise buildings use air conditioning and the windows don't open. In most American developer office buildings the distance from the windows to the core is 40 feet. In European office buildings the distance is 20 feet. They want everybody close to a window that opens. They're into fresh air. That's why European office buildings are slim and ours are chunky. It's the floor-area-ratio difference that makes our system cheaper.

contextual model

opposite:
detail of final design model

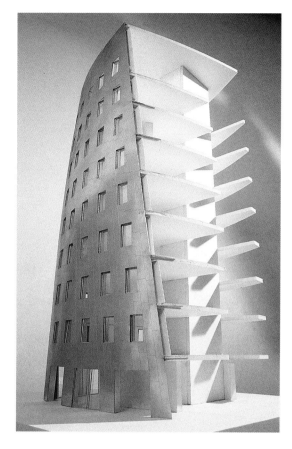

east elevation

north elevation

üstra office building

client: Üstra Hannover Public Transportation

project principals: Frank O. Gehry, design principal
Randy Jefferson, project principal
Eva Sobesky, Randall Stout, Laurence Tighe, project architects
Edwin Chan and Michael Maltzan, project designers

project team: Rich Barrett, Jeff Guga, Ana Henton, John Jennings, Michelle Kaufmann, Naomi Langer, Colby Mayes, Ernest Ross Miller, Kyle Moss, Daniel Pohrte, Jonathan Rothstein, Beat Schenk, Susan Son, Tensho Takemori

197

views of final design model and stainless-steel cladding study

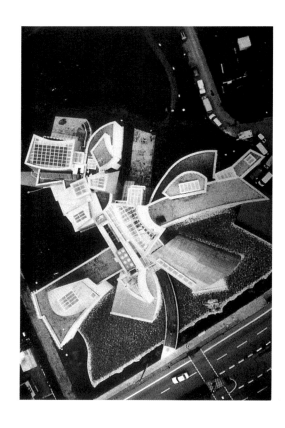

elektrizitatswerk minden-ravensberg gmbh [emr]
communication & technology center 1992–1995

Bad Oeynhausen, Germany

I don't know what a green project is! But I do believe in applying energy conservation technologies if they're viable. In the EMR building it was a consideration because these people are selling energy, and they wanted to demonstrate their ability to do this. So I said to them, "Look, I'm not an expert in this, and I'm not sure what's economically viable and what's wrong and right." When the AIA discovered solar energy and green buildings, all of a sudden the whole bloody AIA was doing so-called energy-saving buildings. They became judgmental and "green."

I was suspicious of the whole thing. But the head of the company is a very nice guy, and I said, "Why don't you bring

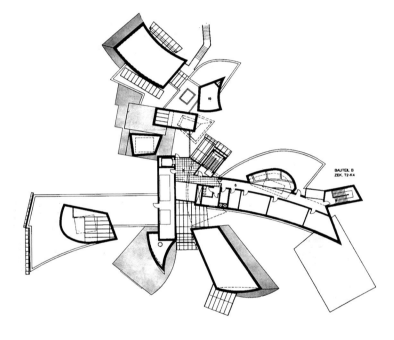

your people here?" He said, "I'll do better. There's an institute in Frankfurt that is leading this thing for the Green Party. They are the state of the art for Germany. I'll bring them to L.A. and we'll have a symposium. We'll work together for a week, we'll discuss all the options so you can learn all about the state of the art." So I met with those four men for one whole week, with my guys. The young kids are always interested. At the end of the week, I realized that Native Americans were way ahead of them.

Heat exchange only works in a residence, not in an office building, because office buildings aren't used at night. If you gather heat during the day to use at night, and there's nobody there at night, you can't use it. There was only one place in the EMR building where they worked around the clock, the control section on the left-hand side. It has a heat exchange. It retains heat gathered from cells in the windows; at night the cells are opened and heat is released.

I said to them, "Why don't we have a bunch of bicycles out in front, and we'll just have people in the community come by when they want to do their exercises. They'll sit on the bicycles and generate a little power, and it will run the building." Craig Hodgetts and Ming Fung designed an exhibition for the building that demonstrates a number of ideas about energy and energy conservation and they put two bicycles inside.

199

the pinwheel plan determined in the early Gehry sketch is also seen in the aerial view of the finished building (opposite), in the second floor plan, and in a design process model

**overleaf:
two views of the EMR exterior and reflecting pool**

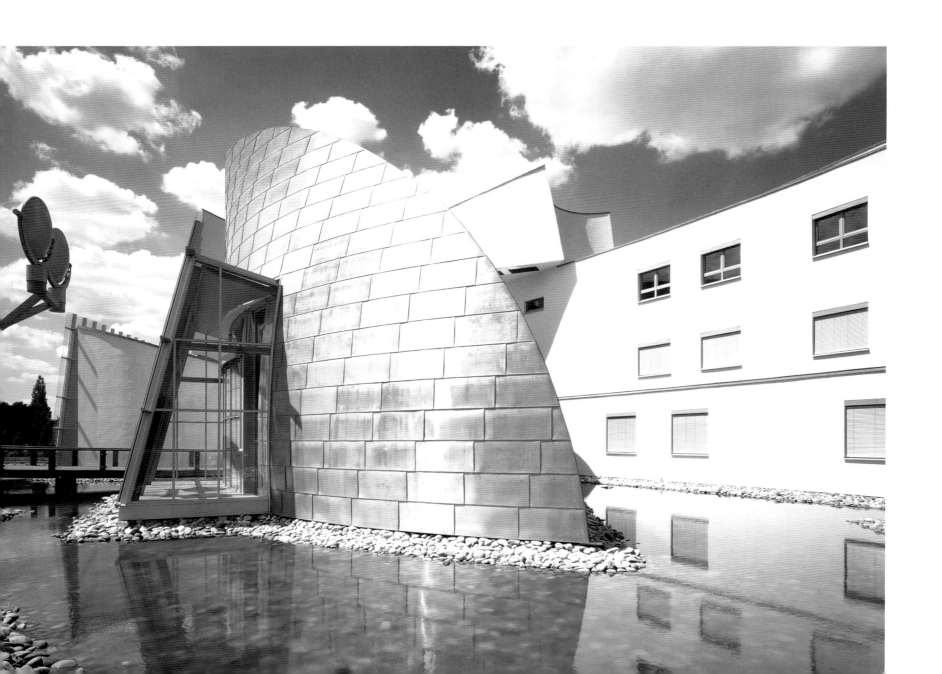

three interiors: skylit hallway, skylit conference area, and Gehry's bentwood chairs in a dining area

opposite:
detail of ventilation duct

For air-conditioning, which is needed only a week or two of the year, we pop a skylight that's right at the top of the roof, and it takes the hot air out. It works like a dream. Native Americans did that, too. I've been doing that for years. The Schnabel house has such a skylight. You push a button to open it and it takes the hot air out. It saves energy, and when you turn your air-conditioning on, finally, when you have to, you don't have to leave it on for a very long time.

The solar stuff works for hot water. It works for pools, but it's expensive. We couldn't use wind, as there is almost no wind there. So after a week of being with these experts, we didn't learn that much. On the ceiling of the auditorium, I used

voltaic cells. I used them because I had a glass roof, and the voltaic cells created a trellis effect, so you didn't get direct sunlight. You have the cracks between the voltaic cells that let light in, and that works.

Cal Tech has developed a thin metal skin that's a voltaic cell. It will store energy. With it, the sun will create electrical energy. The whole skin of a building could be a voltaic cell. To make it, they weave strips of metal, like a fabric. I think you could do it in any metal.

The EMR Communication and Technology Center is a 46,000-square-foot Gehry pinwheel plan, located along an entry road to the town of Bad Oeynhausen, in a district of domestically scaled warehouse buildings. Garden areas are at the north and west sides of the building. The network control center governs regional power distribution. In addition, the building includes an exhibition hall, a conference center, dining area, and an office wing. All are accessible from a two-story skylit interior street. The exterior is a combination of stucco, glass, zinc, and copper on a reinforced concrete structure.

emr communication & technology center

client: Elektrizitatswerk Minden-Ravensberg GMBH

project principals: Frank O. Gehry, design principal
Jim Glymph, project principal
Randall Stout, project architect
Randall Stout, Vince Snyder, Michael Maltzan, project designers

project team: Tomaso Bradshaw, Jonathan Davis, Matthias Seufert, Todd Spiegel, Hiroshi Tokumaru, Laurence Tighe, Tim Williams

detail of main entrance

opposite:
rear elevation

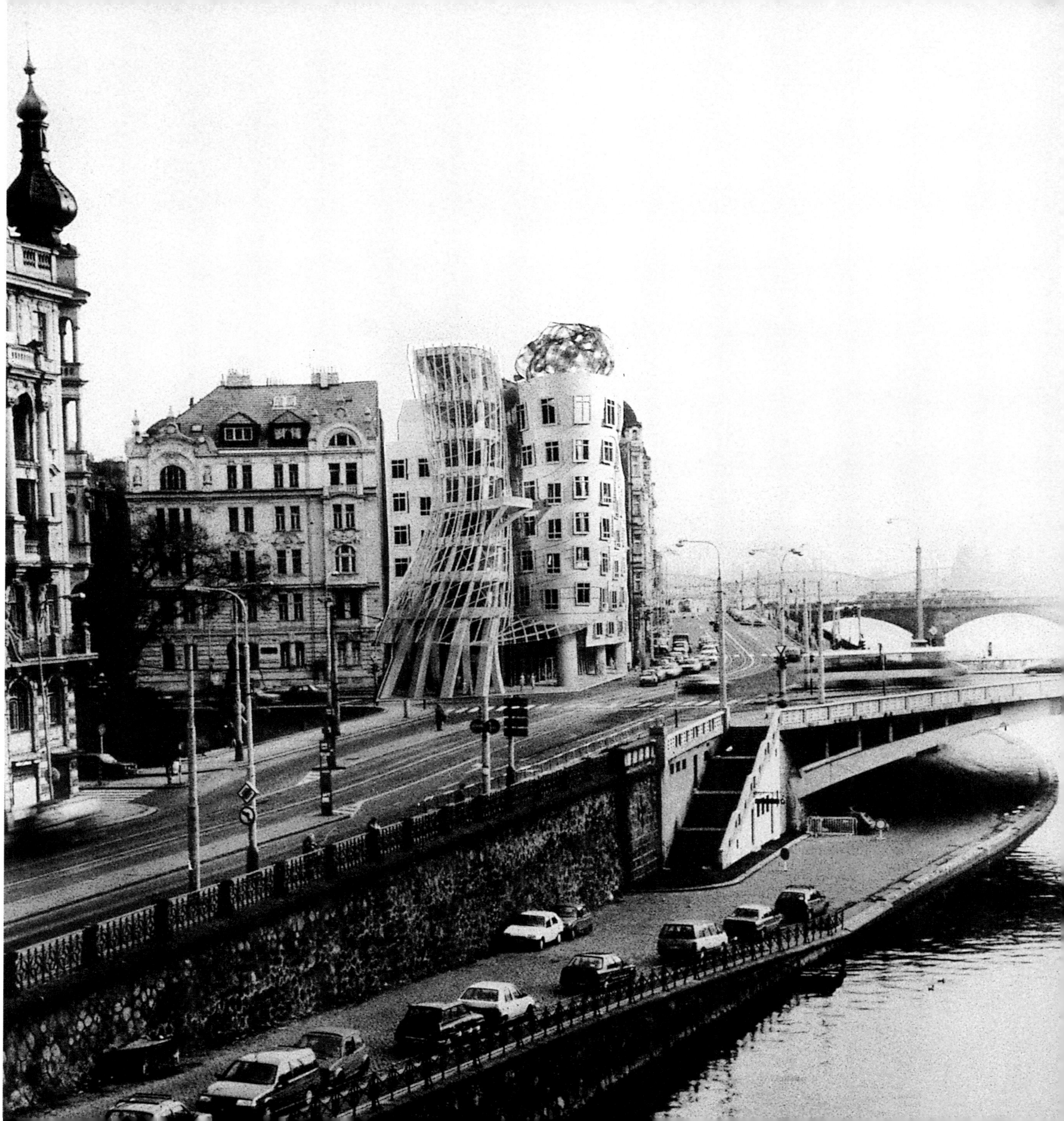

opposite:
collaged process photos of the
building in context; it is referred
to as "Fred and Ginger" by the
people of Prague

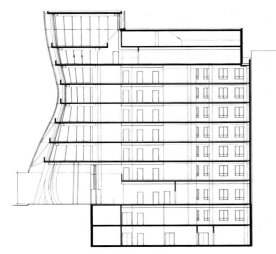

section aa

nationale-**nederlanden building** 1992–1996
Prague, Czech Republic

I can't be an entirely different person when I work abroad. You bring your baggage with you. But my intention is to be part of each place. My effort is to work contextually, but not to pander to tradition. I have other principles: living in my time instead of in the past; interpreting what I see and how I fit. I don't consciously take Los Angeles with me. Maybe I do. I take *me* with me, whatever that is. I think Bilbao relates to there, and Prague relates to there. I wouldn't have done those buildings in Los Angeles.

I spent about ten days in Prague before I started really designing. I went over three times. I had a collaborative architect in Prague, Vladimir Milunic. He knew the ropes. My perception was that in Prague they designed the old buildings with implied towers. They put little caps on top of them and gave them each a hat. That was interesting to me. That was a clue. The other was that in the nineteenth century, the windows and other elements had details that gave a certain texture to the buildings. Even though they looked like they were stone all the buildings were colored plaster. I picked up clues from the plaster, and from whatever I saw.

My building was on a square piece of land on a street next to a river and a bridge. Vlado told me that the city really wanted to aim the street toward the bridge, and they asked if I would do something with the building to project out so that the body language would be there. He negotiated with the city to do that. The developer liked the idea because it gave him a little extra area for the floor plate, which was very small. It's not an economical developer building because of its small floor plate.

The collaboration with Vladimir Milunic was easy, because when I first met him, and they asked me to do the job, I said, "Look, it's too small for a collaboration; don't do that to this guy." And Milunic said to me, "I want you to do it." I said, "Wanting me to do it means I'm going to do it." He said, "I want you to." I started working, and Milunic led me through the city. He talked me through a lot of ideas. I said, "Well, for me, Prague has implied towers, and that is the language of the waterfront." And I thought we should use the implied towers. I thought we should make one tower that turns the corner, to take us into the plaza, and then another tower that fronts on the plaza that also pushes the street out. Milunic agreed with that, and he got it approved. He was very helpful to me in explaining the urban issues that the city was involved with, that they worried about. He didn't get involved with the shapes.

The first Prague model had two towers that were square. One projected out. Then I blended them. Then I decided to make one glass. The first model looked like a woman's dress, and the Czechs made fun of me.[17] They're very proud—they consider themselves to be Europe's intellectuals, especially

207

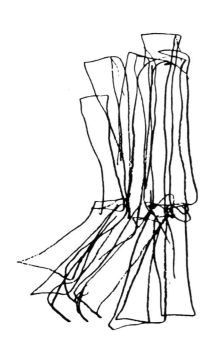

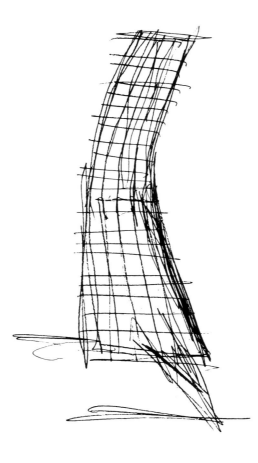

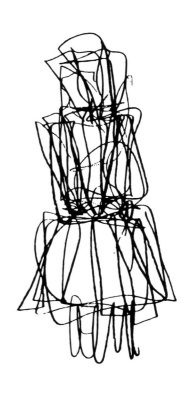

because of Vaclav Havel, their poet President. Milunic spent four years in prison with Havel. They were cellmates. They are really close friends. They understand "abstraction" and they hate postmodernism. When they saw the dress they thought it was postmodernism, and they gave me lectures about abstraction. Even Havel did. They didn't understand where I was going.

I was struggling with the window breakup in the adjacent nineteenth-century buildings that became higher floor to floor. I had two more floors to deal with than were in the existing buildings. If I had just kept the windows flat, you would have read them as two more floors. I worried about that, because it

would have been abrupt. So I thought, how can I make blurry edges so you don't realize that there are more floors? I started making the model, and I started to push the windows up and down. I pushed one up to the top of the ceiling and one down to the floor. Then I built it on the model, and the texture of it fit in, so I knew it was all right. Then I drew the lines to add another layer of texture. That's something I'd never done. I got self-conscious about it after I drew the lines, and I thought, "Well, this is stupid; it's kind of a pastiche—you can't do that." Then I straightened out all of the lines, and they didn't look good. So in the end I said, "Well, my instinct was right, and I don't know why."

 Consequently, someone outside the Gehry office nicknamed the glass tower Ginger, the solid tower Fred.

opposite:
the relationship to neighboring buildings is evident in this photograph showing the arrangement of windows and the sculptural crowns on both buildings

nationale-nederlanden building

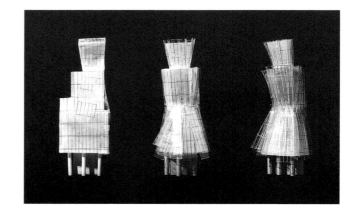

The approach to architecture should be like science, with breakthroughs that create new information, not the repetition of old ideas. For example, we've developed new windows in Prague, in the Berlin bank project, and in Dusseldorf. I decided the windows were like hanging framed pictures on the wall. Instead of being part of the skin, the window is articulated, it tilts, has a presence. I worked very hard trying to devise a window that looked like it was attacking the form instead of eating it away. I thought of it like a swarm of bees coming at a wall.

The module is for one office to have one window. But they didn't do that. They left it, and it really looks good. I wouldn't have thought it would look good, but it really works. The nice

nationale-nederlanden building

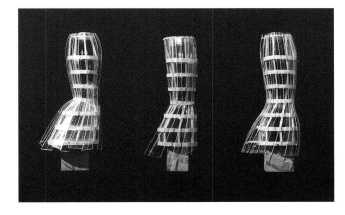 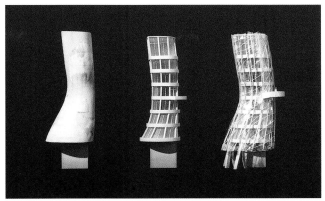

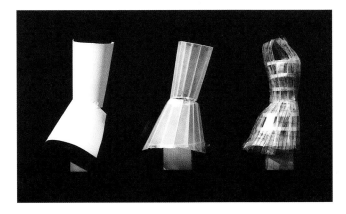

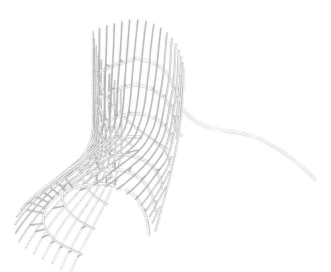

thing is that the glass tower is the conference room on every floor, and each one is a different shape because of the dimensions. It's quite interesting.

I tried to break down the scale in Prague so it would work with the nineteenth century. There it's almost seamless. On one side you come along and you don't realize it's a new building. We maintained the height line. The old buildings have five floors, and mine has seven, so I couldn't just go straight across. That's why I bumped the windows up and down—to blur the difference. Because it's a commercial office building they needed more floors. Five is nineteenth-century floor-to-ceiling, and seven is now.

There was a public referendum on the building before it was built. If you build a dumb, ordinary building, everybody expects that. As soon as somebody does something unexpected everybody gets angry. Nevertheless, we won—fifty-eight to forty-two.

design process models of the evolving glass tower form that were shaped by hand and then used as the basis for the Catia model

nationale-nederlanden building

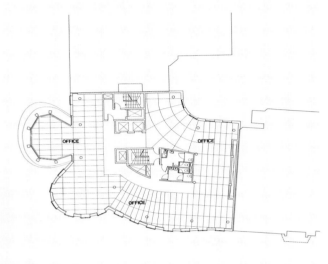

window and plaster façade mock-up

final design model

steel framework for the glass tower under construction and detail of the completed glass tower (lower right)

opposite:
detail of windows on river façade

213

214

finished model of the sculptural
building crown, referred to as
"Medusa" by the Gehry office

opposite:
the sculpture under construction

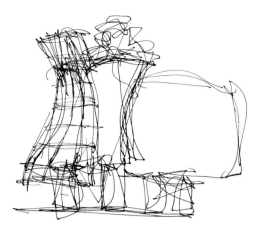

client: Nationale-Nederlanden/International
Netherlands Group

project principals: Frank O. Gehry, design principal
Jim Glymph, project principal
Marc Salette, project architect
Edwin Chan, project designer

project team: Douglas Giesey,
Masis Mesropian, Eva Sobesky,
Thomas Stallman, Lisa Towning,
Philip Rowe, Kristin Woehl

nationale-nederlanden building

Prague's historic district has long been a broad mix of epic styles carefully watched over by the city's preservationist community. The Nationale-Nederlanden Building's site, at a crucial corner along the Vltava River, was a challenging context for Gehry's dancing towers. Guided through the local political scene by Vladimir Milunic, his collaborative architect, Gehry was able to create a joyous landmark carefully aligned with its nineteenth-century neighbors. The glass-enclosed tower is pinched in at its waist to allow residents of the adjacent building a view across the river. The 62,800-square-foot building projects toward the bridge at its corner. The glass tower forms a covered colonnade and a canopy over the main entrance. The ground floor has a café and several commercial spaces. A roof-level restaurant tops the six office floors. The dome atop the enclosed tower is formed of steel mesh strips.

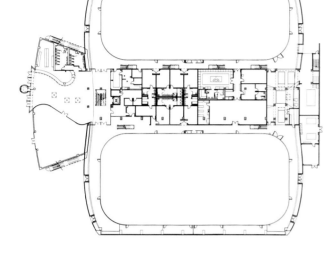

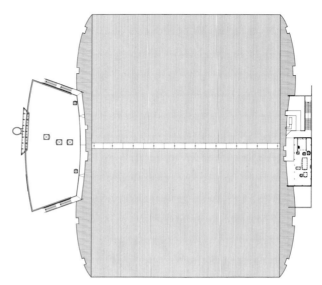

floor plan and roof plan

The interior is better than the exterior. It's a reversal of my usual problem. I put the money there, because I knew I was going to be skating there! A couple of times a year I go there and we have practices. I love the hockey players. They're kids.

I wanted the interior to be like the wooden rinks were in Canada when I was a kid. Most of the hockey players come from Canada, and we've talked about that over time. They all wish they had that kind of rink. I wanted to please them, to make a place that was nice for them. When we started talking about the project and said we wanted to use a wood interior, everybody said, "You can't afford it." It's more expensive than the rinks are now. Most new rinks are just metal Butler buildings with exposed insulation.[18]

It was fun to do. There are things I might have done differently. I could have put windows in where the ceiling comes down to the seats in the middle and then, where it comes down on the outside wall there should have been a skylight. But the worry is that if you let natural light in, it melts the ice. And because I didn't do any of that, they can keep the ice at a very good temperature, and all the skaters love it. It's the best ice in California. The pros love skating there.

This community ice center has a dual function: it is the practice rink of the NHL's Anaheim Mighty Ducks, and it is a neighborhood rink serving youth hockey programs. The double curve of the anodized aluminum roof reflects the two wood-clad interior shells; they are divided by a central lobby that includes a snack bar, skate rental area, and an equipment shop.

 218

disney ice 1993–1995
Anaheim, California

[18] Butler buildings are pre-engineered steel or wood-framed structures.

**opposite:
detail of building façade of anodized aluminum**

220

exposed Glu-lam beams curve
above the ice rink

opposite:
palm trees form a witty ring
around this southern California
ice rink

client: Disney Development Corporation

project team: Stefan Helwig, Gaston Nogues, Mok Wai Wan

project principals: Frank O. Gehry, design principal
Randy Jefferson, project principal
Tomaso Bradshaw, project architect
Michael Maltzen, project designer

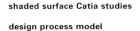

shaded surface Catia studies

design process model

opposite:
conceptual model of rock
formations

telluride residence 1995–
Telluride, Colorado

This is the third house we've designed for Jay Chiat. I don't know if he's going to build it. It's very similar to the plan of the Sirmai-Peterson house. Jay changed sites because the last one had controls that conventionalized the house. Although we made a nice house within the rules, he didn't like it. He was offended by it. So he bought thirty-five acres, and the new house sits in the middle; the next guy is in the middle of his thirty-five acres, and they don't see each other. One neighbor, Dick Ebersol, head of NBC Sports, just hearing the description of Jay's house, sold his lot. He thought it should be a log cabin.

The house steps down the hill. Our inspiration was Duchamp's painting.[19] There is a bedroom and a den for Jay, a living and a dining room, a garage and a mudroom, two kids' bedrooms, and one guest bedroom. It will have a concrete foundation, the frame of the building will be very sculptural, and it will be covered with black copper, which is a roofing material. It's a very animated roof with holes punched in it, which seems appropriate for snow country.

At some point you create unusual spaces when you get very deep folds in the envelope. That's what we're struggling with in Telluride. You can find ways to do it. The other thing is the difference between the inside and the outside. That's very interesting, if you don't rigidly adhere to the idea that the inside and the outside have to reflect each other, like the religion of architecture says it has to—although it never did in the good stuff, anyway. I've been bashed for that a little bit.

223

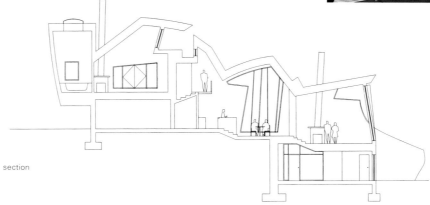

section

design process models

opposite:
model pieces line the walls of
the Telluride work area

telluride residence

rachel allen: The first models are simply a series of wooden blocks that we cut up according to the program requirements and floor-to-floor heights; they form the basic program skeleton. We always start there. This program is really simple. It's a three-bedroom house with a guest house and a den. We started stacking blocks up to try to develop a plan that responded to the site, as it slopes very steeply.

We started the model by getting the blocks as tight as we could and as efficient, and then started wrapping them with paper to make the sculptural shapes. It's miles from anything else, so you don't see anybody else's house, and more important, they don't see us. Edwin Chan, the project designer, once said that you don't know if you have to hide it until you know who's looking. They might want to see it!

After we got this model where we liked it, we digitized it and scanned it into the computer, and used Catia to jump scale and build it. It was really exciting when it first happened. The roof is black copper. It's actually very common on Korean temples and sometimes on Japanese temples. I don't know how they do it. Dipping a copper sheet into an ammonium nitrate bath causes a chemical reaction with the metal.

It's actually a molecular change that is permanent. Over time it looks like clay. It will be terrific against the snow. The house will be like a big boulder. The grating is a departure from Frank's house, with the timber and the projecting prisms. It will have cubist windows.

[19] Marcel Duchamp's *Nude Descending a Staircase*, 1912

upper level floor plan

ground floor plan

lower level floor plan

226

edwin chan: The cubist windows are just a way to see how simple we can make it. I don't think the windows are completely resolved yet. We wanted to see if we could start from the language of Frank's house, instead of the language from the Korean museum, and maybe there's a way to take it to another level. I love the fact that it's a real house. I love the fact that it's out there, and it looks like a mountain; I think that's great.

In May we revised the scheme. We tried to straighten out the building a little bit. The purpose of that exercise was to help us establish some kind of cost model, a better understanding of what it means to build in the mountains, so that we can proceed with it. Unfortunately, it hasn't really helped us that much. The question is that nobody really knows what it means to build the type of building that we designed in Telluride.

The interior is very simple. It's drywall with exposed wood wherever it's appropriate. One of the fantasies we've talked about is that we see this as an opportunity to create a colorful interior that is very soft, in contrast to the exterior. We want to play with fabric, or maybe leather, so that when you come out of the cold, you'd be in a very colorful, soft, warm interior. That was part of the fantasy.

This design walks a fine line between naturalistic forms and architectonic, highly geometric forms. It's an idea that we started playing with in Korea.

structural study model

client: Jay Chiat

project principals: Frank O. Gehry, design principal
Randy Jefferson, project principal
Edwin Chan, project designer

project team: Rachel Allen,
Kamran Ardalan, Rich Barrett,
David Nam

227

Years ago, when I designed Vitra, a man in the advertising business, Thomas Rempen, came to the opening and asked me to design a building in Dusseldorf on the river. For some reason, I didn't respond positively to him. So he asked for another recommendation, and I recommended Zaha Hadid. So they hired Zaha, and they worked with her for four or five years. She did one of her best buildings ever for them. But they didn't build it. It was too difficult.

Rempen kept in touch with me during that five-year period, and he had another job for us to do about three years into it; over time I grew to like him. I'd gone to Dusseldorf a few times to meet with him on another project in the harbor. Then he called and asked if I was going to be in Germany, and could I come by. So I went, and he told me that they couldn't do the Zaha building, and that he had written to her and told her they couldn't do it. There was a new partnership, and they were going to build the building for half the budget. He didn't think that she could turn around and build a building for half the budget on that site and feel good about it. He didn't want to put her through that, so he asked if we would do it. I said, "Well, I don't want to come in and take over Zaha's job." And he said, "Well, we need a building, and you're our first choice, but if you don't do it we'll go elsewhere." It was a great project, and they had already written Zaha a letter terminating her. I thought, we need the work. So I took it. It's three spec office buildings—one metal, one plaster, one brick—with a very tight budget.

It's financially very successful. I was trying to fit into the urban pattern, and leave the riverfront open so that the people behind would have a view through to the river. All the buildings being built there so far have been built as a wall against the river. So all the people behind are being walled off from the river. We decided not to do that. These are spec office buildings. Our client Rempen's offices are going in the middle one. He has an advertising agency. When we started out he only needed one floor, and now he needs the whole building. In that length of time, he's expanded. Because there are three buildings they were leased quickly. When you rent space in one big building, you have to share the identity. In this case, the smaller users could have an identifiable piece of a smaller building. It's a good idea, and it worked. It's anti-Rockefeller Center. This represents the new world we're in. There's more individuality. It's about democracy.

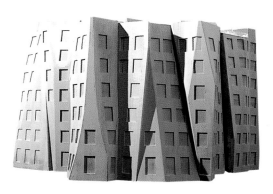

der neue zollhof 1994–1999
Dusseldorf, Germany

construction of mirror finish
stainless-steel wall

opposite:
design process models

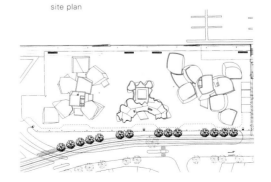

230 **randy jefferson:** The three office buildings are along the edge of the Rhine River. The wall of the center building has a surface whose shape is much like that of folds of hanging fabric. This undulating wall is clad in polished stainless steel, with pre-cast concrete creating the complex shape. For the first time we're using computer data to mill large blocks of Styrofoam that are 2.4 meters wide by 3.4 meters high, by .6 or .9 meters thick, to create the shape of the building full-scale in Styrofoam. Those pieces of Styrofoam become the forms for the concrete. The products of this construction process are pre-cast concrete panels that have the exact shape of the design model transcribed into real life through computer data. They fit together perfectly. This system is more expensive than constructing a flat wall using wood forms, but the contractor is able to recycle the Styrofoam, and the pre-cast concrete pieces fit exactly, even though they're complex in shape.

final site model showing relationship of the three buildings to the river

opposite:
Catia study

detail views of finished buildings

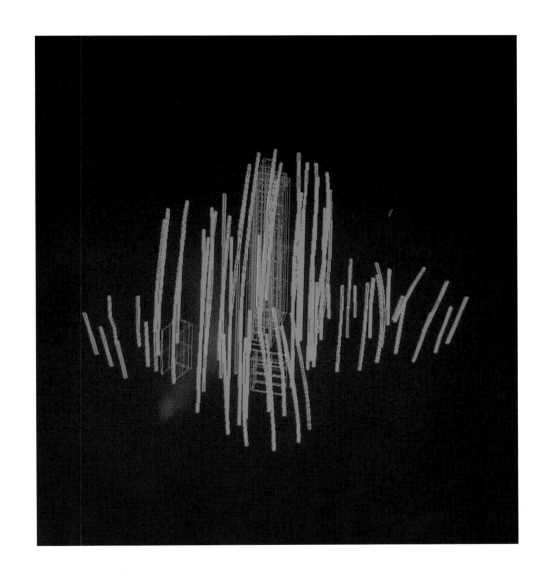

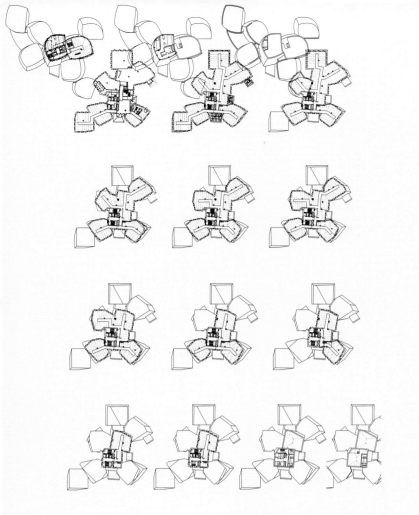

building [a] floor plans

232

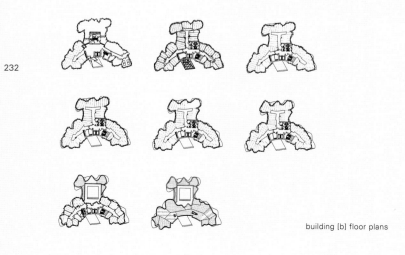

building [b] floor plans

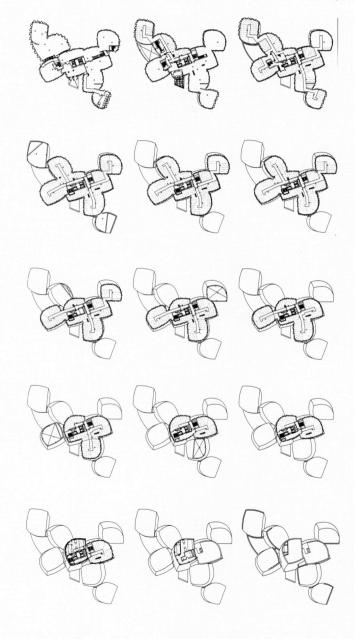

building [c] floor plans

der neue zollhof

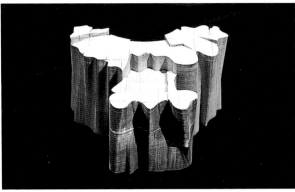

laser-cut models generated
from Catia data

This harbor-front site along the Rhine in downtown Dusseldorf is
part of a broad-based rehabilitation effort intended to provide a public amenity for the city, consisting primarily of art and media agen-
cies among landscaped open spaces. The three buildings encompass
300,000 square feet of commercial office space. The central building
is clad in metal, the east tower in plaster, and the west tower in brick.
Identical operable windows are used on all three buildings, giving
them a visible relationship.

axonometric
looking southeast

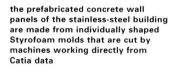

the prefabricated concrete wall
panels of the stainless-steel building
are made from individually shaped
Styrofoam molds that are cut by
machines working directly from
Catia data

detail of stainless building
showing angled windows in
the façade

234

client: Kunst-und-Medienzentrum Rheinhafen GmbH

project principals: Frank O. Gehry, design principal
Randy Jefferson, project principal
Craig Webb, project designer
Terry Bell, Tomaso Bradshaw, project architects
Brent Miller, Lisa Towning, Kristin Woehl, project coordinators

project team: Jim Dayton,
John Goldsmith, Jeff Guga,
Michael Jobes, Naomi Langer,
Joerg Ruegemer, Charles
Sanchez, Bruce Shepard, Rick
Smith, Eva Sobesky, Tensho
Takemori, Laurence Tighe, Scott
Uriu, Flora Vara, Jeff Wauer

der neue zollhof

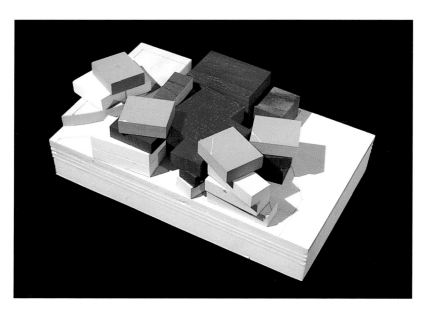

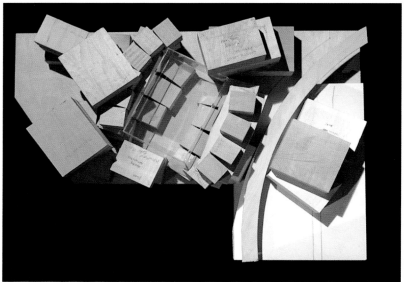

experience music project [emp] 1995–
Seattle, Washington

craig webb: Through the process, we've had disparate elements, chunks of individual buildings. Then we did a model that wove the materials together, which we liked a whole lot, but Paul Allen didn't like it. So we agreed to go back to the individual pieces with individual colors. We're looking at creating overlapping glass strips on the exterior. The glass is like Prague and Bilbao. It won't be visible inside. It's flowing over the top of the metal pieces. We've always wanted to try to weave the individual pieces back together, and the glass is accomplishing that.

It becomes a kind of decorative element, which is something that's bothering a lot of people. It is definitely another layer of skin, but it's not keeping the water out. It's the next layer up. And we're using it for signage. We're looking at using colored glass to mediate

I'm still interested in objects in a field, like villages, but I don't see that idea rigidly applied. I think you can see it in the Experience Music Project, where I started out with separate blocks that the client, Paul Allen, liked. That's the village. If you look at the first models, I was making it more coherent. He didn't like it. He liked the models where I broke it down. I did too, actually. And when I broke it apart, I liked what was going on. I didn't achieve it in that model. Essentially, the building is a one-room warehouse with exhibits inside, and that makes it difficult to break down.

My working process is an evolution, like watching paint dry. This is where I get in trouble with misconceptions about how I work. Nobody realizes that I cut it off at the working drawings and stop. During the front end it evolves. And I tell everybody in advance, "Look, I'm starting here," I show them all the models from the last project. I say, "You look at it, you do it, you listen. I get input, I regurgitate, I move—that's it." I asked Paul Allen why he came to me, what did he want; he said, "swoopy." So my first thought was, "God, he must have been looking at the Bilbao project." I asked him if he'd seen the Bilbao project, and he said no, he'd not seen it. So I asked, "What did you see?" He said, "Well, I don't know." He couldn't tell me. So I said, "Well, the next time you're in my office, would you come in and look at the models, and tell me what swoopy means to you." So he walked all around the office, and he saw the horse's head [in the DG Bank project], and he said, "That's swoopy." I said, "I'm very delighted that you think that's swoopy and that's where you want me to go, because that's the farthest-out I've been, and that's about where I am, so I'd like to take off from there." So then we made models.

I wanted to do something colorful because of the guitars. I immersed myself in the folklore of Jimi Hendrix, and his music.[20] But I told them up front, "This isn't my thing. I listen to Haydn." I'm not a stodgy guy, but I said, "When it comes to this stuff, I'm a pure dilettante." I said, "I'm going to have to get educated." Craig Webb plays the guitar and Jim Glymph plays the guitar. They know all that stuff, so they brought it all to me, all the books and the records, and I listened. I asked Paul Allen if I could use that kind of music for inspiration, and he said, "Yes, that would be wonderful." So those first models were blue and green and we did a whole series of them. Some were too swoopy, some were not swoopy enough, one was just right.

early design process models

between the different colors in the building, and then we're going to light it at night so that it blurs and creates some kind of movement on the surface.

We're creating pipes, which are going to run the length of the building. They're like guitar strings. A lot of people think it looks like the neck of a guitar, with the frets on it. Frank took the guitar neck and said, "Make a bunch of these." We made a

whole bunch of wood slats, and they fanned out so there was a big fan all the way through the whole piece, and it started to undulate, like music. He was trying to get the building to look like music, because of the way it was undulating. So we're going back to that.

You enter the building through a glass key, which we call the "jelly jar." It is a glass weather vestibule. The building

has two orientations. The front door faces the amusement park. Parking is on the side, and so a lot of people are going to come in the other door—which is the second entry—go through this interior street space, and go to the lobby. There is a bookstore, with two shop windows that can be looked into from outside. A visitor can go into the shop without going into the museum. That's true of the restaurant also.

[20] The building is dedicated to the memory of the Seattle-born rock musician. Paul Allen was inspired by Jimi Hendrix's creativity, and he hopes that the EMP will provide inspirational experiences to its visitors.

I found a weird way of communicating with him about swoopy, and we made fun of it, and I'd joke with him about swoopy. He's very shy. I thought it was very endearing actually. I thought it was wonderful. He criticized some of the things, and then I made a model that had the broken pieces—the yellow and the black and the blue thing. I showed it to him, and he said, "Oh my God." And I thought he hated it. I don't know whether he loved it. But he's funny. He sees things at a presentation when it's too late to change anything. I was presenting the project at the Seattle Center, and that's when he came to see it, when I was presenting it. What could he do? But apparently, he loved it. He approved it. I told him what I thought was wrong with it. I said I thought it looked like broken crockery, it really was too fragmented. I said, "The basic idea is here, and I want to study the materials. I want to study the terrazzo, I want to study the metals, I want to see what we can do on the budget."

If you look at that first model, it had metal slivers all over it, and broken wires. But he said, "What are you going to do with that?" I said, "No, no, don't worry. This is how I work." I said, "I just throw the idea on, and now I'm going to figure out what to do with it." And I worked hard trying to integrate the thing, and we got somewhere. It was really beautiful. I started to use the metal in a painterly way, where it started to move through. It wasn't all one piece. There was gold and silver threading together. The thing got messier on top, the metal became bigger moves. I was really happy. I think it would have been better than Bilbao. It was on its way. Then he called and came in, and he said, "Whoa! This isn't about what I approved. This is messy." I said, "Well, rock-and-roll is messy." He said, "Well, this is what I approved. I don't know about that." He was very upset. I said, "Look, Paul, you're paying for it. I'm willing to go back to square one, but it will take time. You've got to articulate what you don't like." And he was pretty clear about what he didn't like. He liked the separate pieces; he could understand them diagrammatically. I said "Look, I'll go back and revisit the whole thing." So I did. I dove into this thing. It was a new language, and I got with it, and I started to make inroads. I like where it's going; I'm really proud of it."

EMP has several materials, stainless and painted metal. The stainless is in three finishes: shiny with a purple haze, which is like Jimi Hendrix; the angel hair, which has a little texture; and the gold. The red is painted metal, and the blue is painted metal, and the red will fade. We did that on purpose, so the red will look like an old truck, a faded old red truck. I believe it's going to be wonderful.

We're just starting to develop the casework and the retail specs. Then there's a metal wall that goes all the way through: It's weaving all the materials together in a way that's not happening outside. The metal will be the same as the outside. It will probably be perforated for acoustics. There is a café on two levels, which will also have a lot of performances going on. There's a small stage above and a bigger stage below.

There's a curved wood canopy over the top of the bar. It's rock-and-roll! It's a real restaurant. We just started working with the man who is going to operate it. There's a small stage for a singer and two or three other musicians. It's a huge restaurant. It will seat about 250 on the first level.

The second building entry is for tour groups—school children and so forth. In a room called the *Electric Library* they're going to have interactive computer stations where visitors can query the EMP's database. They're trying to work up a system in which you'll be given a set of open architectural headphones, called near-phones. They don't cover your ears. When you walk in front of an exhibit you hear the sound; if you walk away, it's gone. You'll also have a hand-held device that is going to read either bar codes or some other device on the exhibit cases. You will be able to swipe a wand across it that will cue an audio sound track. There's another button on that device to store a particular exhibit. You will be able to go to the *Electric Library* and put it into the computer; it will open the database at that point so that you can get deeper into the exhibit.

There are two classrooms underneath, and a 200-seat auditorium for film series and lectures.

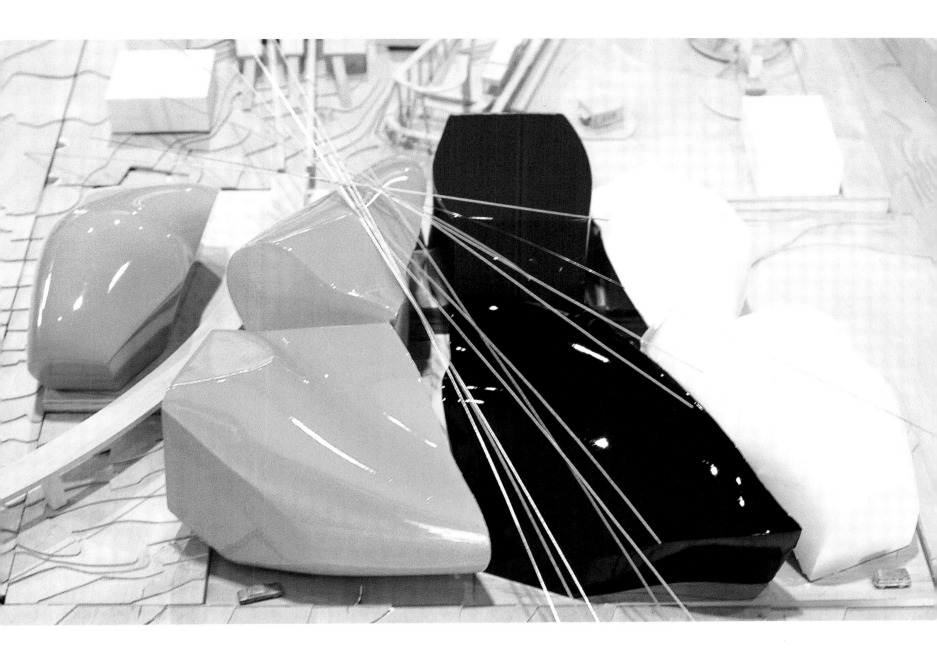

There is coat-check, ticketing, and an orientation space where you get your hardware. The music interactive exhibit is called *Sound Lab*. There is another element that's somewhat similar to the horse's head in Berlin. We're looking at covering it in mirrored stainless steel so that you can walk under it and around it, and everything animates.

Below there are going to be plasma flat-screen video displays that will give you information about ticketing and programs. There will be a whole series of ticketing options, so you can decide to go to a movie or go to a concert or go here or there. *Sky Church* is an area we're not doing. The terminology comes from Jimi Hendrix. He had an idea of a thing he called *Sky Church*, which was a communal space where people would come together and make music, get together and communicate. So they've picked that up as the name for the space. In the normal museum day it will be an entry space, sort of a greeting space that you will come into and go from there into the other parts of the exhibit. They're also going to use it for performances, so it will be for big concerts. Digital Domain, the special effects house that did the film *Titanic*, is creating a multimedia show. There's going to be a pre-show area, and then a platform and probably a big surround screen and other pop-down screens. Paul Allen wants to be able to give people the experience of being a performer on the stage. There's a part on northwest music, there's a part that's more general rock-and-roll, and different eras, rock-and-roll and some roots, so there's a bit of blues. They're also going to go forward into hip-hop and rap.

There's one exhibit that's called *Here and Now,* which is supposed to be the most contemporary music. They're going to try to pull it in on a very frequent basis.

above and opposite: design process models showing the evolution of form, material, and color distribution

opposite lower left: site model

roof plan

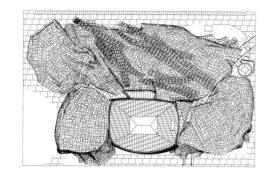

240

experience music project

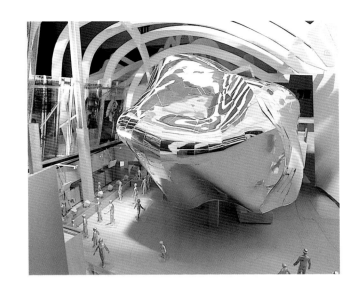

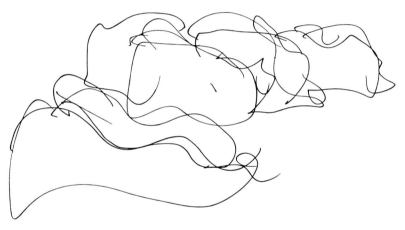

sound lab, demo area section

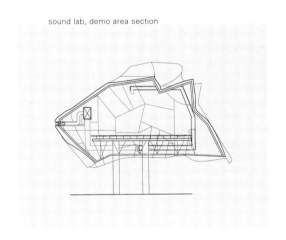

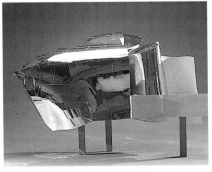

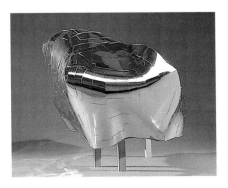

sketch and series of design
process models of the sound
lab demonstration area

opposite:
design process model

large-scale interior models are
created to study the entrance
and bookshop

242

Located near the Space Needle at Seattle Center, the 140,000-square-foot Experience Music Project is a celebration of American popular music and the culture that is its stimulus. Through a variety of interactive programs, visitors will learn about music history. They will experience music through classes and performances, and understand the significance of artists such as Jimi Hendrix, whose innovative music was the inspiration for this project. The building exterior is a combination of voluptuous metallic forms in vivid blue, red, gold, and silver. A 65-foot-high cubic foyer has a blank façade that will be used as a video screen and a backdrop for outdoor concerts. The Seattle Center Monorail, built for the 1962 Seattle World's Fair, provides transportation from downtown Seattle; it runs right through the building. A restaurant, bookstore, and administrative areas are on the ground floor; support spaces and storage are below grade. The EMP is scheduled to open in 2000.

ground floor plan

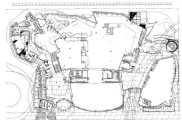

first floor plan

mezzanine floor plan

second floor plan

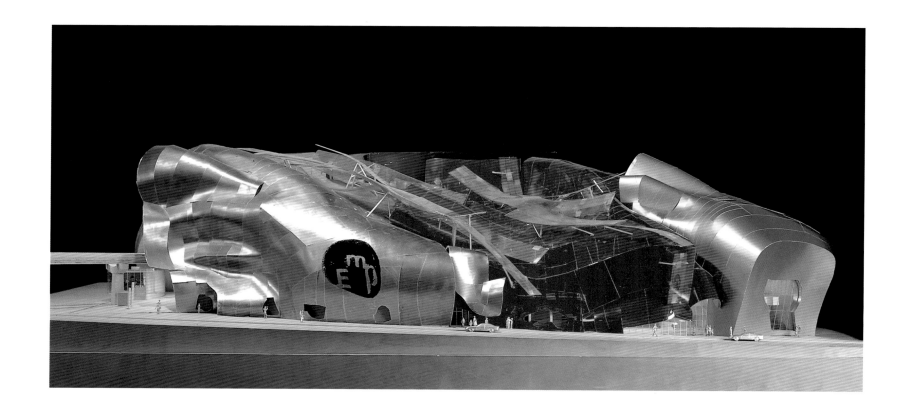

244

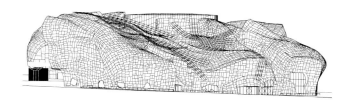

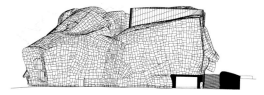

east elevation

north elevation

south elevation

experience music project

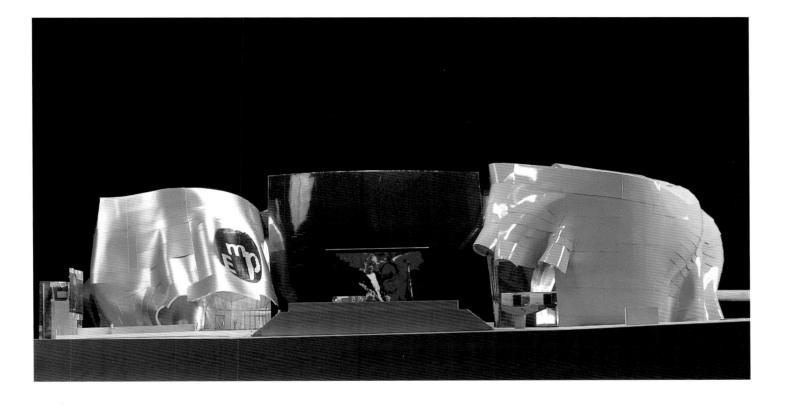

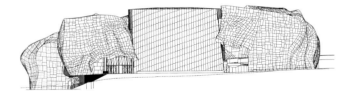

west elevation

**above and opposite:
final design models**

client: Experience Music Project

project principals: Frank O. Gehry, design principal
Jim Glymph, project principal
Craig Webb, design architect
Terry Bell, George Metzger, Laurence Tighe, project architects

CATIA modeling: Douglas Glenn,
Bruce Shepard, Rick Smith

project team: Kenneth Ahn, Kamran Ardalan, Rich Barrett, Herwig Baumgartner, Elisabeth Beasley, Anna Helena Berge, Kirk Blaschke, Karl Blette, Rebeca Cotera, Jon Drezner, Jeff Guga, David Hardie, Leigh Jerrard, Michael Jobes, Naomi Langer, Gary Lundberg, Yannina Manjarres-Weeks, Kevin Marrero, Brent Miller, Gaston Nogues, David Pakshong, Douglas Pierson, Steven Pliam, Daniel Pohrte, Paolo Sant'Ambrogio, Christopher Seals, Dennis Sheldon, Tadao Shimizu, Eva Sobesky, Randall Stout, Tensho Takemori, Lisa Towning, Scott Uriu, Jeffrey Wauer, Adam Wheeler

245

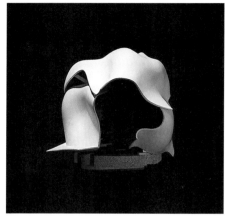

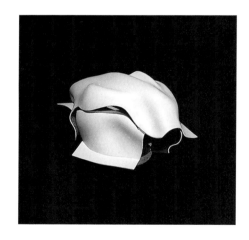

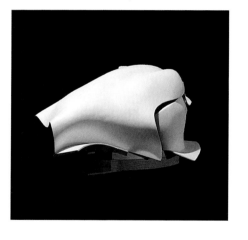

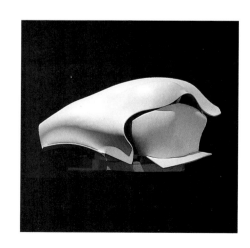

246

The horse's head for the Pariser Platz mixed-use building, part commercial, part residential, came from the Peter Lewis house. The reason it got to Berlin is that we came up with a plan for the atrium with the conference center in the middle—an obvious scheme. A lot of architects have done that. It's not a very original strategy, but it's a comforting thing, a nice strategy. I started to play with the space, and I realized I couldn't solve it in time for the competition. I had this beautiful horse-head shape here and it worked, so I adapted it and said, "We'll change it later, they're not going to like it, but at least it's a finished thing and it will look finished." So we put it in and they loved it, and we won the competition. I stuck with it and refined it, because I loved it, too. I think that Claus Sluter was a big influence there.

The exterior of the building is limestone to echo the Brandenburg Gate. The stone is four inches thick because the Gate's stone is also very gutsy. They want to link all the buildings on Pariser Platz, so we said, "Okay, if you really want to do that, just make the building of thick stone." The bank guys loved it, although it has cost them a lot of money to do it. The scale of the moves I made on the façade of this building relates to Pariser Platz. The other new projects on the square, which are trying to be copies of the nineteenth-century buildings that used to be there, look pastichey, and they miss the point; they didn't learn. There is a hodgepodge of those buildings next to the Brandenburg, but I think ours is going to be the only one that looks right. Because the atrium is enclosed I could use wood on the walls, which you wouldn't normally be able to have on a high-rise building. The offices all have balconies overlooking the atrium. We have a seven-story high-rise wood building inside instead of the steel and marble typical of most contemporary atria. The bank and apartment exterior façades are all stone. The roof is glass.

Several years ago I met the structural engineer Jorg Schlaich, who I think is the best structural engineer alive. He does very thin web, lacy glass roofs. I'd seen one, and I asked him if he'd work with us on this. He taught us that we could make many different shapes. We didn't have to do it the way everybody else does it. He gave me lots of leeway.

The building has a basement, below street level, and we made a courtyard down there too. We had to separate it, because it's a cafeteria. They call it a casino. That's where the

dg bank at
pariser platz 1995–2000

Berlin, Germany

detail of design process model
showing conference room, glass
roof and floor

opposite:
studies of conference room
referred to as "The Horse's Head"
by the Gehry office

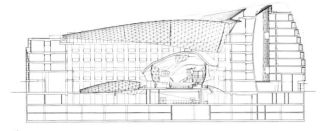

section a

247

employee restaurant is. They didn't want the noise coming up, so we put the same kind of glass roof on that, and we cut paths through it. The paths come to the stainless-steel–clad horse's head, which is a conference area. Underneath it is a theater for movies. This facility will also be rented out.

The apartments are really nice. There's an almond-shaped atrium on the apartment side that goes up through the whole building. The elevator is glass enclosed.

Both sides of the building are joined to other buildings. One side is the American Embassy; the other side was Albert Speer's studio. Speer's bunker was under the site. When they dug down to it they found a dining room table with food and dirty dishes on it, and a few things knocked over. It looked like somebody had just run out of there. When the Germans discovered it, they destroyed it in fifteen minutes. There was no architectural historical review board that came in and said, "You have to save this place." Actually, when they started scraping the grounds, there were bombs, live bombs on the site. They bumped into one, so they cordoned off the area and got the bomb squad in. They got them out, they did it all, cleaned it out, they left, and a few hours later they bumped into another one and they were back!

The bank is really an adventuresome client. We've connected really well with them, and they've made it clear that they really

sketches of "The Horse's Head"

opposite:
final design models and detail of chandelier studies by the glass artist Nikolas Weinstein

a series of glass roof study models

dg bank at pariser platz

want me to see it through my way. We won the competition with the horse's head, and then we talked to them about it, and they liked it, so we didn't change it. We made it better, because it was something we'd appropriated from somewhere else—which I don't do that often. I don't think I've ever done it. I loved the shape. So I changed it.

Gemini wants to make a limited edition of the models.[21] When I made the fish lamps, I felt good doing it. I never thought of them as sculptures, competing with Richard or Claes. I was into the material thing of the glowing color core and the fish images. Crossing the line between architecture and sculpture is something that's been difficult for me.

[21] Gemini is a pioneering print-making workshop in Los Angeles where many artists have come to explore the possibilities of traditional as well as technologically innovative printmaking processes.

 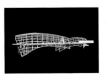 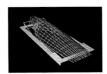

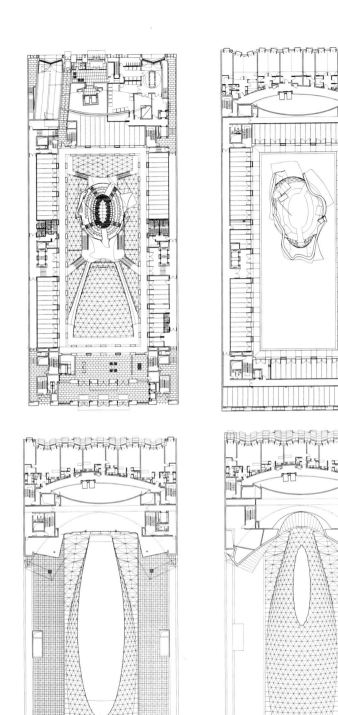

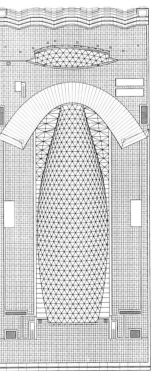

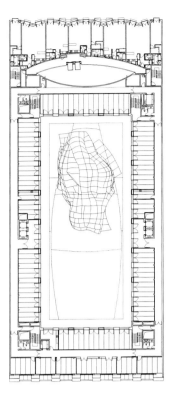

top left to bottom right:
ground level plan
second level plan
fourth level plan
sixth level plan
seventh level plan
roof plan

**final design model of
"The Horse's Head"**

**opposite:
design process model
of roof structure**

250

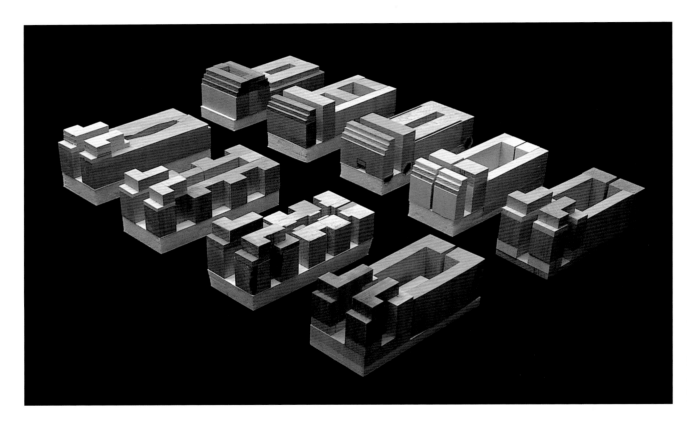

programming studies

opposite:
design process model and details
of the housing area facade

252   **randy jefferson:** If you have a piece of paper or a sheet of metal, and you bend it into a cylinder or you bend it into a cone, that's fairly simple, because you don't have to stretch it. But to make a piece of metal conform to the shape of a surface that is complex in the sense of a sphere, the sheet of metal must be stretched. The conference hall shape in the atrium of the Berlin project is clad with stretched stainless steel, two millimeters thick. The pieces forming the shape are approximately two by four meters, though some are smaller than that. In this project we're using the computer data as the source of information from which the manufacturer can stretch the metal. We've been fortunate to find contractors in Germany who are building the hulls of ships with thick steel plates and fiberglass hulls, such as those for the twelve-meter boats built for the America's Cup races.

Pariser Platz houses the five-story Berlin headquarters of DG Bank, which faces onto Pariser Platz and the Brandenburg Gate; some thirty-nine apartments, rising to ten stories, are located on the south side of the building. The façades are clad in buff-colored limestone, as is the Brandenburg Gate. The 200,000-square-foot building's large atrium has a curved glass ceiling and floor and contains the main conference hall, whose stainless-steel horse-head-shaped form appears to float within the deep space of the interior. The residential part of the building has a smaller atrium that provides natural light for both sides of each apartment.

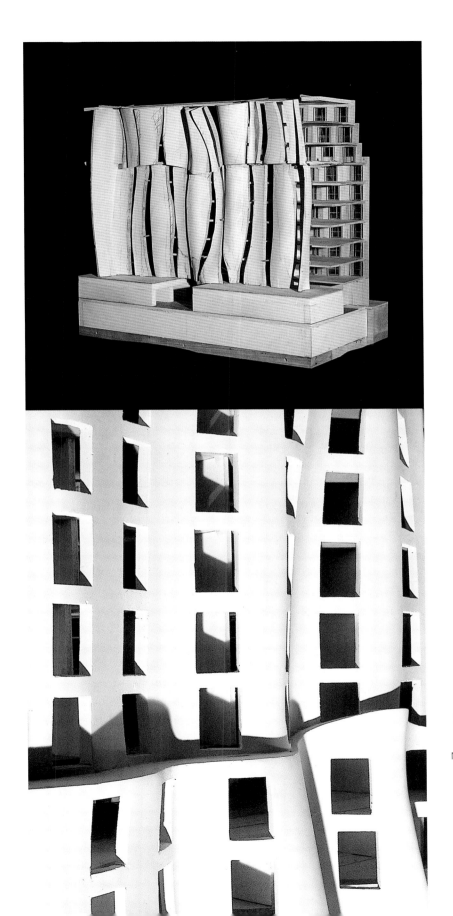

north exterior elevation

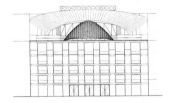

south exterior elevation

client: Hines Grundstucksentwicklung GmbH
DG Immobilien Management GmbH

project principals: Frank O. Gehry, design principal
Randy Jefferson, project principal
Craig Webb, project designer
Marc Salette and Tensho Takemori, project architects

CATIA modeling: Bruce Shepard, Rick Smith

project team: Kirk Blaschke, Nida Chesonis, Tom Cody, Jim Dayton, John Goldsmith, Jeff Guga, Leigh Jerrard, Michael Jobes, George Metzger, Jorg Ruegemer, Tadao Shimizu, Eva Sobesky, Laurence Tighe, Scott Uriu

254 **condé nast** cafeteria 1996–
New York City

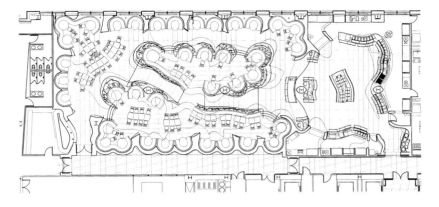

floor plan

The whole project started because the client, Si Newhouse, is very interested in architecture. His wife, Victoria Newhouse, is an architectural historian. Condé Nast's offices will use the entire new office building that was designed by the New York firm Fox and Fowle. The publishers asked us to design all the interiors, but it wasn't a job I wanted. However, we accepted the cafeteria project. It was a very ample budget, and when you have clients truly interested in architecture, who want to do something special, you start pushing it.

We decided to go with the scale of the fourteen-foot-high room. I tried a lot of schemes, which broke the room down into smaller pieces, but in the end I liked the proportion of the room as one big space. I decided to make privacy implied by using glass walls like curtains, curtain shapes that seem to be blowing in the wind. We made an island in the center that is surrounded by glass curtains that are really beautiful shapes. What makes them beautiful is that each shape is different. It would be easy to make a repetitive shape, but that would be another thing. So each shape is different, and you have to consider how to mold each shape. Normally they would mold glass like that over stainless steel. With the computer you'd make a stainless-steel mold, then slump the glass onto it. Each mold would cost $20,000 or $30,000. That would have blown the budget. So we started doing research with the glass people, and we found a way to do it with a fakir-like bed of nails that adjusts to various shapes, like the children's toy. (You've seen those toys with movable pins; you put it on your face and it makes an impression in the shape of your face.) The glass panels are being fabricated like that. We expected that maybe ten percent of the glass pieces were pushed too far, and we would have to change them and be a little more conservative. We were expecting that, but that hasn't happened yet. They engineered the ten most complicated pieces, and they say they're okay.

The rest of the space is blue titanium. I was looking at pictures of Giotto's Arena Chapel. Well, when you're in a room that's enclosed, you think of sky—"How do I get some sky in here?" And the light blue does something nice. There are a few windows on one side, but that's all. So we've got to get light in, and the blue titanium suggested sky, and it was new, it was something I hadn't used, and everybody liked it, it's beautiful. It's on all the walls and the ceiling. And it's perforated because of the acoustical requirements of a cafeteria. We didn't want the room to be live.

There are some private dining rooms as well. They are very special molded glass and wood. I'm trying to design a chair and a light fixture for those rooms. The tables are made of Brazilian granite.

The 260-seat Condé Nast cafeteria is intended to provide employees with a convenient lunchtime dining and meeting facility. It includes a main dining area, a servery, and four private dining rooms. In the main dining room, booths that accommodate four to six people are distributed along the perimeter walls that are clad in perforated blue titanium panels with acoustic backing. Additional booths are located on a raised platform that is enclosed within curved glass panels in the center of the main dining area. Freestanding tables and chairs, to be designed by Frank O. Gehry & Associates, will be distributed throughout the main dining area. The servery, which is adjacent to the main dining area, has stainless-steel countertops, blue titanium walls and canopies, and ash veneer floor and ceiling. The walls, floors, and ceilings of the four private dining rooms are ash-veneer plywood. Curved glass panels articulate the east wall of each room. Three of these rooms have movable partitions, allowing them to be transformed into a variety of spatial configurations for special occasions.

**design process model of
chandelier for private dining
room (above)**

**opposite:
design process models**

condé nast cafeteria

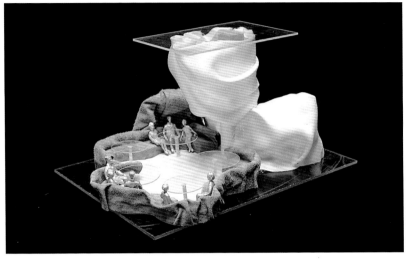

edwin chan: The booths in the cafeteria will have a quilted naugahyde finish. The shapes evolved from some of the exploration that we started in Bilbao. There, we were able to create shapes from Frank's sketches. In order to make the dining room acoustically absorbent, we have to make the titanium perforated. It will be in pieces, so you will see lines as well as perforations. The glass-enclosed island will provide the right kind of intimacy, and at the same time you'll be able to see all of the activities going on around the island. The glass curves are like figures, like people, because of the exaggeration of the forms. They have a lightness and sense of movement. The floor is wood as is the base of the glass island. It's the ash that we used in Bilbao. There will be four private dining rooms apart from the main cafeteria area. Those floors will be carpeted. Ash wood walls will be on one side, and on the window side there will be formed glass similar to the glass in the cafeteria; however, this glass will be translucent rather than clear.

condé nast cafeteria

final design models

client: Condé Nast Publications, Inc.

project principals: Frank O. Gehry, design principal
Randy Jefferson, project principal
Edwin Chan, project designer
Christopher Mercier and Michelle Kaufmann, project architects
Leigh Jerrard, job captain

computer modeling: Douglas Glenn,
Julian Mayes, Bruce Shepard,
Rick Smith, Kristin Woehl

project team: Kamran Ardalan,
David Nam

259

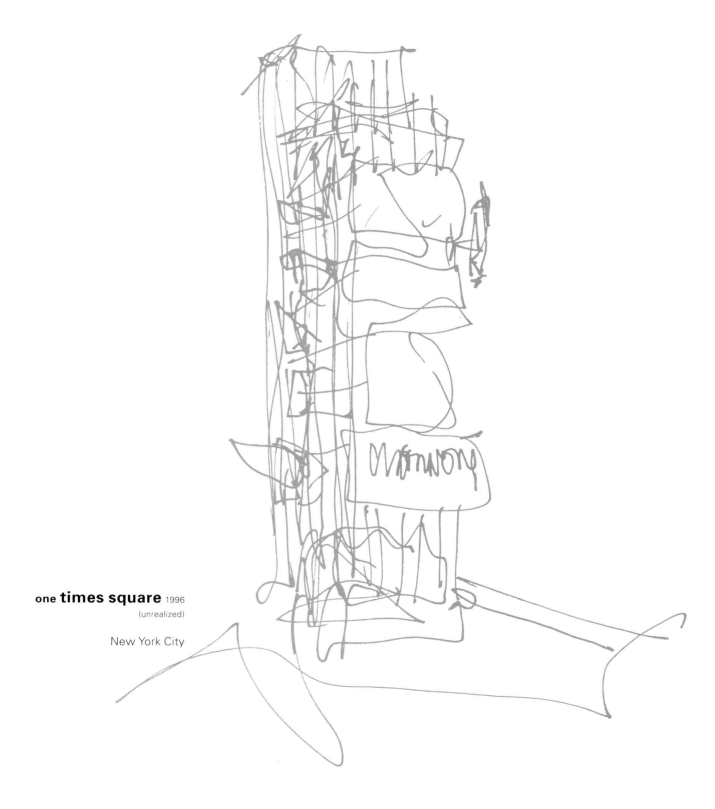

one times square 1996
(unrealized)

New York City

A friend at Time Warner asked me to do something with the old New York Times building at 42nd and Broadway. The purpose of their renting the building was to put a store on the ground floor. Up higher in the building they were going to locate a restaurant and a bar. But the building is kind of useless; it gets all its rent from billboards. They had the funny idea that if I could remodel the building, I would somehow figure out how to make the Eiffel Tower out of it. God knows how many people go there every New Year's Eve to watch the ball come down.

Time Warner people came to the office and I said, "I think it's a job for a graphic designer or an advertising copywriter, somebody else; it's not a job for an architect." They said, "Well, we want it to be an architectural job. We want you to do it. We know you're going to come up with something." So I said, "But what if I don't? Because I know when I accept an architectural commission I can come up with something. But this," I said, "I'm insecure, I'm not sure, I can't guarantee you." I said, "Who is your boss?" They said, "Terry Semel and Bob Daly." I said, "I want to tell them and see what they say." So they said, "That's fair enough." The next day Terry Semel and Bob Daly came to my office, which apparently they'd never done for anybody, and they arrived upstairs and they sat down with me and said, "We really want you to do this."

As I was talking to them, I remembered the Sid Caesar-Imogene Coca cuckoo clock on television. There was a show in which Imogene and Sid were dressed up like two Swiss guys—characters in a cuckoo clock. They came out and they'd bong the bong, then they'd go back inside, presumably once every hour. Each time they came out they did the prescribed thing. At first there was a little glitch; eventually it degenerated until it became a brawl—they started beating each other up, hitting each other over the head. A real Punch and Judy! That image came to mind while I was sitting at my conference table with Terry Semel and Bob Daly. And I said to them, "You know, I just had an idea. Wouldn't it be wonderful if Time-Warner turned that building into a cuckoo clock, and Bugs Bunny could come out, Elmer Fudd could shoot him, you'd get a puff of smoke like the Camel ad." And I said, "At night from one in the morning until six in the morning the building could be snoring," and I said, "Batman could come out at midnight and fly around the building, Superman could come out for lunch." They loved it.

I said, "That's not architecture. It's a funny idea, it just came to me." And I said, "If you like it, take it; it's yours. You've got all the technology and people to do it." And Semel said, "Oh, come on, we want it to be more than that. We want you to capture the building and make it up." So I started to work on it seriously. I brought in the people who do Skylab with the arm in space, and I got all the technology, the special effects guys. I got everybody in and I figured out we could do it. But then we could only project three feet from the skin of the building. I kept getting stuck, because you couldn't do anything architecturally that would deal with those signs. I couldn't figure it out. I struggled with it for several weeks, and finally I gave up. I said, "Look, I can't do it." I said, "Here's a scheme. Here's where the store should

design process models

go; it should go on the bottom, and this is how it should go; here's where the restaurant should go; and here is the cuckoo clock. But I don't know how to enclose it. And the conventional ways of doing it don't appeal to me. I don't want my name on it."

I called them. It was a Thursday night and I told them all of that, and they said, "Please, try one more day. We'll come tomorrow afternoon. If you're really tapped out, we'll let you off the hook." So I went to bed that night, and I woke up at three in the morning, and I realized that the mesh could be the skin and that it could move. We had contacted one of the big zoning lawyers in New York. He told us that if it went in and

out, if whatever the skin was made of could move back, you could do it. That's when I had the dream and that's when I came up with the idea. So the next morning I called Edwin Chan in, and I said, "Get some screen wire and let's play with it." That's when those images came up. So we called Terry Semel and said, "It worked, you're right, we have an idea that we think is pretty good; we'd like you to see it." He came with Bob Daly. We set it up theatrically. We made the building smoke. Superman came out. We showed him the whole thing. They were ecstatic. They danced around the model, and they told us what geniuses we were. And they got in their limo and left. We've never heard from them again.

262

One Times Square is located on a triangular lot between 42nd and 43rd streets and Broadway and Seventh Avenue in Manhattan. Designed for the New York Times in 1904, the building would later become the site of an annual rite, drawing thousands of visitors to Times Square to watch a motorized ball drop from the roof of the building heralding the start of the New Year.

In 1996, Warner Brothers signed a long-term lease for the entire twenty-five-story building and retained Frank O. Gehry & Associates to renovate the building and create a major symbolic presence in Times Square for Warner Brothers and its parent company, Time

Warner. Because the building's usable floor plates are extremely small, due to the unique triangular geometry of the site, the client rejected the idea of producing a traditional office building. The program proposed for the building by Frank O. Gehry & Associates involved the creation of an open public plaza directly accessible from Times Square. A Warner Brothers retail store would be located below grade and a theme restaurant and bar would be located on the top levels of the building. At the center of the open public plaza, a sculptural glass form would mark the entrance to the below grade retail area, which would be accessed via escalators. The restaurant

and bar would be reached via express elevators located on the exterior of the building. The building was stripped of its neo-Gothic detailing in 1966, and the white marble that currently covers the façades of the building would have been removed. The exposed structural skeleton would be covered with a translucent metallic fabric that would keep the existing billboard signage intact. A computerized program was proposed to create an hourly urban spectacle on Times Square.

client: Warner Brothers

project principals: Frank O. Gehry, design principal
Randy Jefferson, project principal
Edwin Chan, project designer/architect

project team: David Herrera, Leigh Jerrard

detail of translucent
metallic fabric

opposite:
final design models
with metallic fabric
and Superman

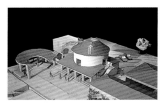

duval center at
st. monica catholic church 1997–1999

Santa Monica, California

We are creating a two-level chapel, a cloister, and a glass porch open to a terrace that will tie the chapel together with the church's main entrance at a side aisle, and create a place for outdoor activities. The pastor would like to add an exterior shrine. The current chapel scheme has a rectangular first floor and circular second floor. The church has a red tile roof and a stone facade.

The pastor was pretty scared when he saw it, so it ended up looking a little bit Firenze. It's my Florentine period. You can say I had a lapse. But it's going to be nice. It's Berta's church. I had to go to the 9:30 mass and the 11:30 mass to present it one day. That was funny. The 9:30 mass is for the younger people who go early. I got a standing ovation. All the old fuddy-duddies were at 11:30 mass. They applauded, but no standing ovation. No bouquet for me from those guys.

There's going to be a fountain. And I am secretly hoping that we can have it named for Berta's mother. I made a front porch for the community room. When they have services, they come out and they sometimes serve cookies and lemonade. Then there's a room upstairs for meetings. And kids use these rooms. I would have pushed it a little further, I guess, given time, but it's already under construction. The Bishop got nervous with it, even as it is. He'd never seen anything like it. I had pushed him beyond his comprehension of the building, and he's just now beginning to understand. It's just a million dollars. That's what you get for a million dollars.

They're going to try to convert me. They're already trying.

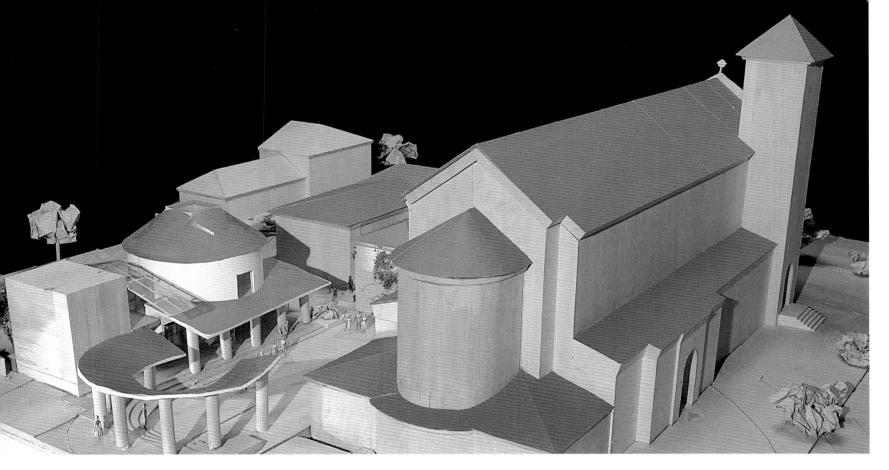

I run into people in Santa Monica from the parish, and they say, "Man, you're a hero." I'm not interested in the Catholic church, but I am interested in the art that it produced. Better than the Jews. You can see that in Israel. The Arabs look better than the Jews—times ten. I guess that the genes are always there. But if there are no role models, it doesn't happen. The period we came out of is a period of revolutionaries. Jews are that. So if you have a left brain-right brain (whatever brain we have) mentality, then that's what you do, and if you have that revolutionary experience, you'll go fight for it. That's what's happened. It leaked out the edges. I think they were always there, in my opinion. That's what I said when I was interviewed by the *Jerusalem Times* about ten years ago, because we had meetings with Jerusalem's mayor, Teddy Kollek. I love Teddy Kollek. But he doesn't have a visual thing, and he thinks all architects are the same. So if your name is architect, you're the same. It's the guy that did that terrible building over there. So he points and he says, "Why do you do things like that?" I say, "I didn't do it."

So the *Jerusalem Times* asked me what I thought about new architecture in Jerusalem. I said, "When a kid comes home from school and tells his parents he's going to be an architect, and the parents support it like they do when the kid comes home and tells them, 'I'm going to play the fiddle,' then architecture will become good. Until you do that, it isn't going to happen."

The St. Monica Catholic Church complex includes an elementary and high school, a convent, a rectory, a conference center, a pastoral center, and the existing Duval Center, which the Gehry plan will replace with a new building. After demolition of the multipurpose building, a 3,550-square-foot multipurpose building will be constructed with a first-floor classroom opening onto a porch that leads to a new patio area. The patio forms an open-air extension of the church and serves as an additional meeting area for mass or after mass activities. It is protected by two canopy elements supported by round columns. The second-floor meeting room is a rotunda with a central skylight. An outdoor stairway covered by a canopy is north of the main building. The terra-cotta tile roofs on the rotunda and the canopy utilize the language of the existing context and unite the Duval Center with the entire complex.

client: Church of St. Monica

project principals: Frank O. Gehry, design principal
Randy Jefferson, project principal
Terry Bell, project architect

project team: Thomas Balaban, Yannina Manjarres-Weeks, Mok Wai Wan

**above and opposite:
final design models**

Leon Botstein, musicologist, conductor, head of Bard College, is the client. This project started in a funny way. There's a gallery in Sun Valley that has a fancy art show and a party on New Year's Eve, and everybody who lives in Sun Valley comes to it. They asked me to be in the show. They said they would pay for my family to come to Sun Valley and spend a week. We went, and while we were there, I rented the hockey rink for two sessions, private sessions with the kids. We were looking for a pickup game, so we let the word out that we had the rink. A man came and asked if he could play with us. He said he was captain of the hockey team when he was at Yale. A lot of people came. We had a really fun game.

Then they all came to that New Year's thing. And the guy who played hockey for Yale saw my work for the first time, and there were some books of my work there. I didn't pay much attention. A few weeks passed after I got back to L.A., and one day he called and said, "I'm a trustee of Bard College, and I'd like you to come there and talk to us about a project, a student union, a small student union." I went to meet them. Berta went with me. They picked us up in a car and drove us up there, and we had lunch with Leon. He said he really didn't want me to do a student union, it was too small a project, and he really wanted to build a small concert hall. There was no competition or anything. He just said, "I want you to do this."

He had done his homework—he was ready. He said, "If you don't do it, I won't do it." So we accepted, of course; it was a beautiful project. There were several site options. We liked the site that was in an old section of campus, with the administration building and several others. If you built a concert hall or a little performing arts thing, it would make a village of it, and it would be kind of beautiful. So we proposed that, and he didn't like it. He liked the idea of it, but he said that's not what he was doing this for. He explained that there were pedagogical issues, and that he wanted the building to relate to the art school, the dance school, and the theater school—to the existing arts facilities. He said, "While it makes sense as a village, that's not what we're here for." And he said, "I have to think about it in terms of how it's going to fit into the curriculum." So he made it go near the existing arts buildings.

You couldn't argue with him, even though architecturally it didn't make good sense. That's come back to haunt him now, because the neighbors are objecting to where we're putting it, because they can see it from a wildlife trail. They mind seeing it because it's not a tree. It's near another industrial looking building, which is sitting in the trees. So that led to making it a facade, just dealing with the foyer, and letting the back be more industrial. We thought that would help us with the budget. But Leon wants to be able to put a hundred or so musicians on the stage. If he did a modest concert hall for sixty musicians, the volume of the room could be smaller. If you go to a bigger volume it ups the cost.

And then he brought in the director Joanne Akalitis one day, and she said, "This doesn't function as a theater; it's not going to work." I said, "Well, we were designing a concert hall, what do you mean?" Well, he started talking to her about it as a theater. So we found things out suddenly. It makes sense for a school to have a dual-purpose hall. But it makes no sense architecturally. Sound problems create added costs. Then there's a fly gallery, and then there's a full orchestra pit for opera. Joanne is going to make operas with Leon. Anyway, it will be an experimental place like no other. And it will be okay for dance; it will work like the Joyce Theater. It can be reconfigured for small productions too.

It's modest. If you straightened all that stuff out, if you made a box out of this whole thing, you'd save about a million and a-half dollars, less than ten percent of the total cost. But that always is the case. The "decoration" I call it, whatever we do as architects, is usually less than ten percent of the building. For Disney Hall it's ten to twelve percent, Bilbao it's ten percent.

The materials are as cheap as we can build it. The main box of the building is concrete, and it will be exposed both outside and inside. The floor of the auditorium is concrete. So we added wood on the ceiling; the panels are acoustically molded. The balconies are wood and the acoustical shell, where the orchestra sits, is wood. That will make it pleasant. But it's not expensive. It's not fancy.

All of the back stage, from the proscenium to the back, is all just matter-of-fact, as simple as you can make it, probably plaster. I wanted concrete block like the other buildings, but it was too expensive, so it's going to be plaster. The roof and the foyer and the surround of the hall are stainless steel. The U-shaped foyer surrounds the concert hall, so you walk around the balconies to go into the concert hall. It was easy to make

bard college center
for the performing arts 1997–

Annandale-on-Hudson, New York

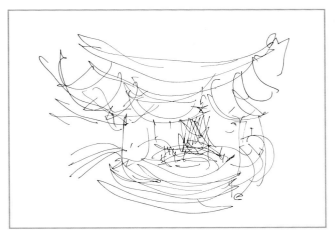

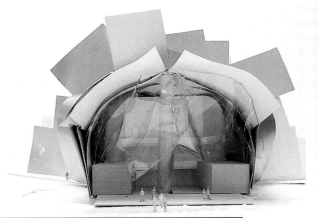

an interesting shape in the foyer, because you don't have the acoustical issues there. And we made what I called a hand-kerchief over the entrance. It's probably the only decorative piece on it. The front part of it is a canopy. The back part goes up and houses a skylight, which brings light into the foyer. And the idea is that the foyer becomes an amphitheater, an out-door amphitheater, with steps going down through the entry. The foyer can be used as a stage in the summer for meetings and discussions with students, and it gives them just a little extra learning or teaching space.

Because it sits in the trees, and it's all green and wonder-ful, we're able to use stainless steel, which is cold and maybe forbidding in other places. We think that because of the envi-ronment, it's going to look okay. In fact, we tried titanium, which is warm, and it started to look funny. It looks overdone. It becomes decorative in the trees, for some reason. Anyway, that's our perception. So using stainless steel is a little tougher look in the setting.

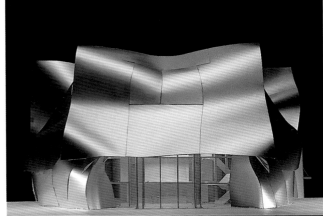

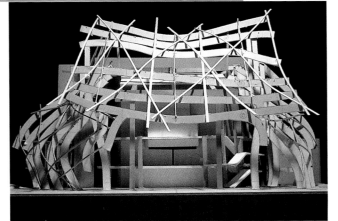

**sketch of hall interior; design
process model of hall exterior;
final model of hall exterior;
structural study model of hall**

**opposite:
new site panorama**

section aa

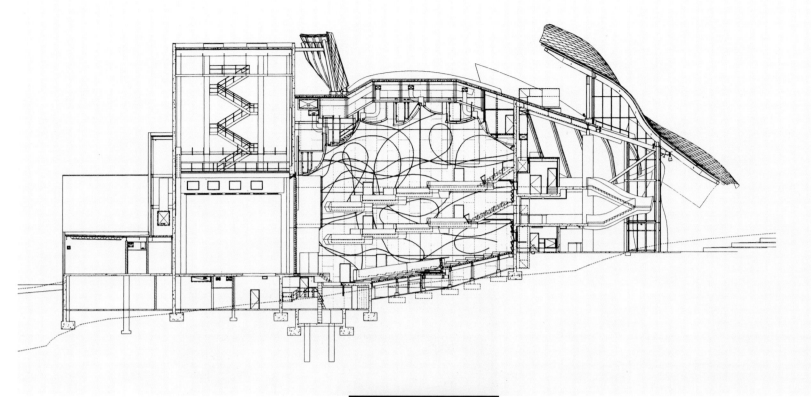

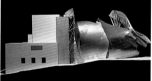

stage level plan

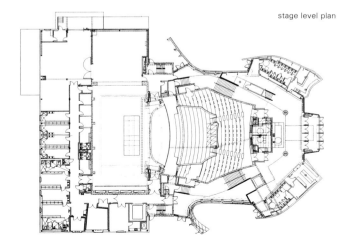

bard college center for the performing arts

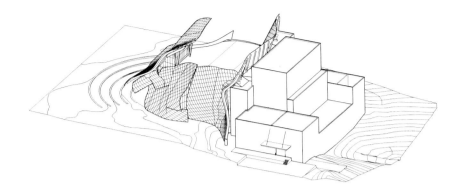

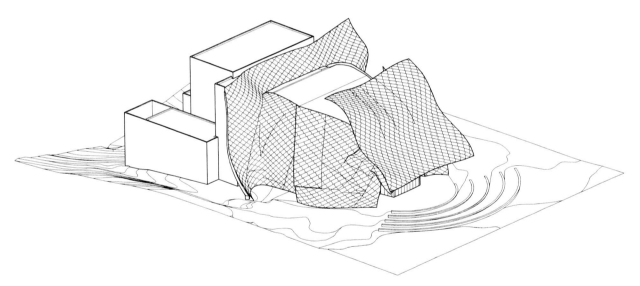

exterior axonometrics

This 60,000-square-foot hall will provide performance space for opera, dance, drama, and music. The multipurpose auditorium will have a full fly system for opera and drama, a wood concert shell, and forestage lift for symphonic music. The house will have an orchestra section and two balconies, a wood ceiling, and concrete walls and floors. The entry façade will be stainless steel; the other façades will be plaster.

opposite:
design process model of exterior

design process models of
hall interior

client: Bard College

project principals: Frank O. Gehry, design principal
Randy Jefferson, project principal
Craig Webb, project designer
John Bowers, project architect

CATIA modeling: David Blackburn, Julian Mayes

project team: Kirk Blaschke, Nida Chesonis, Matt Fineout, Sean Gale, Jeff Guga, John Murphey, David Pakshong, Yanan Par, Lynn Pilon, David Rodriguez, Tadao Shimizu, Jose Catriel Tulian, Mok Wai Wan, Yannina Manjarres-Weeks, Adam Wheeler, Brad Winkeljohn

design process model of site

opposite:
design process models showing
gradual evolution of concept

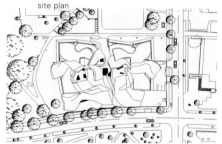

site plan

**the weatherhead school of management
at case western reserve university** 1997–

Cleveland, Ohio

Case Western is the legacy of the Peter Lewis house. When he decided not to build it, he gave fifty million dollars to the Guggenheim, and he gave fifteen million dollars to Case Western, and hired me as the architect. Peter said he did both of those things because of the house. He has since given another nine million dollars to Case. Our building is going to cost thirty-five million, so they need to raise an additional eleven million.

Peter has a relationship with Case, because he hires their graduates, and he also lectures at the business school. That is one of his true loves, and where he's truly expert. So he has a very strong relationship with that school. Since Lewis is giving most of the money, it's all set in motion. It's part of the Weatherhead School, and Al Weatherhead is there, and so it will be called the Peter B. Lewis Campus of the Weatherhead School of Management.

I think the building is one of the best things we've done, because it's circumstantial. We worked hard trying to get a flowing quality in the metal on the Korean museum project, and we got pretty close. When that project died, and Case ended up with a high part and a low part, I was able to use that idea again. But because I'd worked it all out on Korea, I was able to take a leap forward from Korea.

As in every other project, in our basic analysis we studied the classrooms, the offices, and the needs. It's a graduate

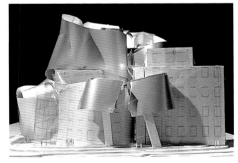

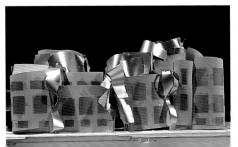

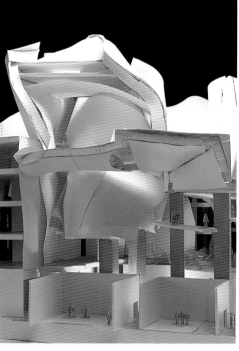

school of business. We have tons of models showing a great deal of the furniture, the layouts, and everything. This is an important process. There's a model of each office with the furniture in it, and there are models of all the different classroom types with all their configurations—oval, square, etc. As I start manipulating the shapes, the scale of the shapes is related to the clarity of all the research. It allows you a lot of freedom for expression (expressionist architecture, I call it), to be able to manipulate those forms. Because of the computer, we know the quantities we can afford. Some of the models look very voluptuous and way-out. They're overblown, they are not economically feasible, but they do relate to the programs. Then, slowly, you start. If you were writing a treatise, you would write too much, and then pare it away. It's the same with these buildings. You pare away the stuff and get down to the essence of it. And because we have the computer monitoring it, we know what the economic essence is, and all we have to do is correlate that with the visual essence. And when you finish, it all fits. It's like a Swiss watch. But it looks like you just threw it up in the air and it lands. That's what I like the most, to maintain spontaneity while responding to specific needs.

The classrooms are placed all around the building with a maximum of interaction between students and faculty. In the middle area, we doubled up the classrooms. We've piled them on top of each other, and that leaves bumps in the middle. The reason we've put that in the middle is that our building is the first building on campus that's overscale, because the president took away some of the land and made us go a story higher. We had to up the density because they were running out of land and they had to preserve land, and the next batch of buildings was going to have to be at this higher density. Unfortunately, we were the first one. When you do an expressive building, and you're bigger than the guys next door, you look overpowering. So we took the wedding-cake strategy of pushing the high part into the middle, so there's a transition. That led to those bumps, and the classrooms piled up in those bumps. There's a bump that has two classrooms in it, and there's a space between the walls that's like a crevasse. It's kind of like Glen Canyon, Arizona, but it's more studied than that. I haven't gone to that naturalistic thing yet. Maybe that's the next step. (Jay's Telluride house starts the process. It looks like rocks. I think nature is a good model for us.)

272

entrance level

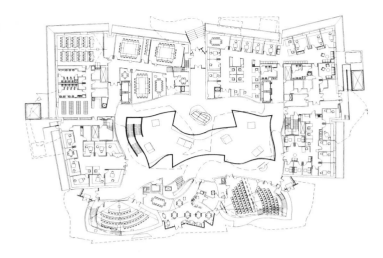

lower classroom level

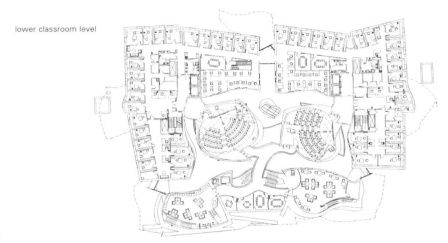

The outside will be brick for the base building, if we can afford it (we're struggling), with an option for brick and plaster. We prefer brick because the rest of the campus is brick, and the brick has some shape to it, too. We started out with solid, four-square brick. But as the roof was formed, the steel part, we started to blend the brick pieces into it sculpturally. We build big models to check costs and form.

This 143,000-square-foot building will house the Weather-head School of Management. Exterior materials will be either titanium or stainless steel panels, hand-set brick, and glass. The highly sculptural, metal-clad exterior surfaces will face away from the campus toward the street. Exterior brick surfaces will face toward the campus and neighboring buildings. At the points where the metal panels and the brick meet, the brick will pitch inward in a slight curve in response to the metal.

The interior of the building will be plaster. The walls of the communal spaces within the interior will be highly sculptural. As these walls rise toward the roof of the building, they will play off one another and respond to one another, creating a series of dramatic, narrow, ravinelike interior spaces. Skylights will allow slivers of natural light to filter down through these spaces. The ground floor of the interior is dominated by two freestanding, sculptural shells (called "Buddhas" in house) that rise toward the roof of the building and rest atop large sculptural columns. Two lecture rooms are located within each of these shells. Communal spaces, including a library, meeting areas, and lounges occupy the remainder of the ground floor. Additional classrooms are located on the basement level, in a semicircular arrangement. Administrative areas, offices, and meeting areas for professors and their staffs are located on the upper floors along the periphery of the building.

273

the stone walls of Glen Canyon, Arizona were inspirational to Gehry as he developed the Weatherhead design

opposite:
large-scale study models
of interiors

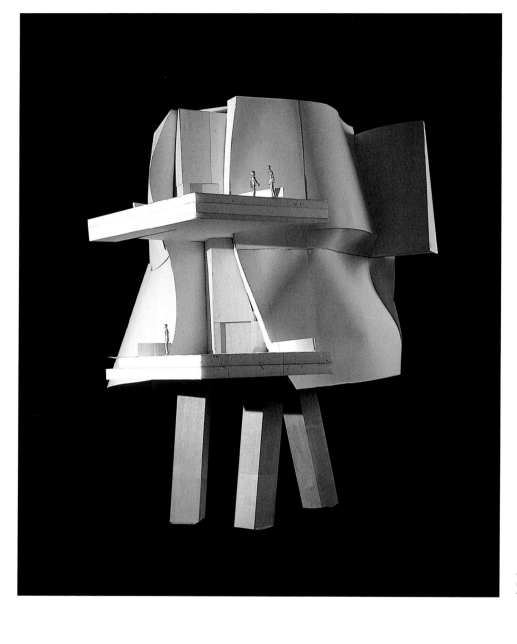

classroom model studies
referred to as "Buddhas" by
the Gehry office

274

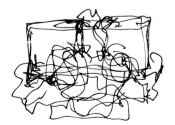

the weatherhead school of management

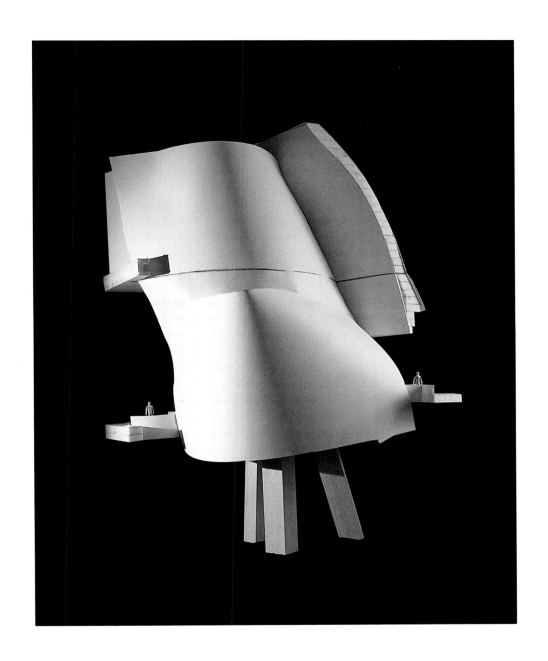

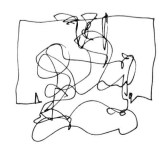
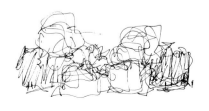

276

**final models indicating the
relationship of the metal and
brick building elements**

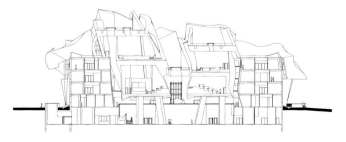

section at atruim

the weatherhead school of management

client: Case Western Reserve University
Al Weatherhead School of Business

project principals: Frank O. Gehry, design principal
Jim Glymph, project principal
Edwin Chan and Douglas Hanson, project designers
Gerhard Mayer, project architect

CATIA modeling: Julian Mayes, Brian Papke, Rick Smith

project team: Rachel Allen, Thomas Balaban, Steven Brabson, Henry Brawner, Heather Duncan, Matt Fineout, Bryan Flores, Jason Luk, Christopher Mazzier, Frank Medrano, Robyn Morgenstern, Yanan Par, Jonathon Rothstein, Marc Salette, Frank Sheng, Derek Soltes, Friedrich Tuczek, Frank Weeks

stata complex at
the massachusetts institute of technology 1998–

Cambridge, Massachusetts

This MIT project is essentially a huge office building to be named for two donors, so the building has to have two identities. One section is for artificial intelligence—robots—and the other is for the philosophical group of the linguist Noam Chomsky.

What excites me about the project is dealing with the scientists. Also, it's a piece of MIT that has historical significance. It is the replacement for Building 20, which the scientists loved because it was like a warehouse; they could do anything to it. The users want that to happen again, and I want that to happen. The university set up criteria to prevent that from happening again because they say that the building is only on loan to these departments, and twenty years

279

later somebody else may be there.

Anyway, it's going to be fun to work through. How to attach it to the MIT system, how to solve the problems of the scientists, how to deal with the quadrangle of MIT in a way that represents a different way to look at it than the stodgy old way. They have this thing called the "Idea of the Infinite Corridor." All of their buildings are connected underground; you can move internally through the whole campus. There aren't very many distinguished buildings on that campus. They want this one to be special.

Before they hired me, I predicted they'd all want what they had, and that's exactly what they said in the first meeting. They said, "How do you break out of what we're used to?" We said, "Well, you try things; you start things." They said, "Like how?" So that's when we said, "Let's try a number of ways to organize the staff offices and the shared spaces." And we did, and got them involved. Some of them hated it and they sent us e-mail. Some of the ideas really bothered them.

One lady was all over me at one of the meetings saying you can't do this and you can't do that. I said to her, "If you think I'm here to take you out of your banal office, which is poorly lit, poorly furnished, has poor acoustics, and poor natural light—if you think I'm here to take you out of that in order to put you into something that really works, with user-friendly

280

rachel allen: We've made a circular diagram for the clients. Blue represents the underground service tunnel system that the students use at MIT to get around in the winter; red represents public access; and yellow represents the inter-users circulation. We also have a quarter-inch model of the same scheme. We're going to build the whole building at that scale right away so that we can study it from the

inside out before we start shaping the building.

It's a dollhouse thing. The clients love that because they can understand what's happening. They are surprised at the box shape, but they don't believe that it's really going to be a box. They know better. We tell them that it's not going to be a box for long. There are four departments that are divided into two main categories. The Laboratory of

Computer Science is the higher tower, and the lower tower, which is connected to an existing building, is the Artificial Intelligence Lab, which has all the robots. The Linguistics Department is connected to the Computer Science Department, through the notion that computer language is a language in the first place.

We've lifted up the grade about twenty feet and put a main

lobby on the campus side. When we lifted the grade we created a plaza area for the students. The lower quadrant is public, and the upper terrace is a more private sort of Philosophy Garden for the scientists. All the colored blocks represent different conference rooms for the different departments. And the red block is the café. It's a quiet dining terrace. All the common areas for the different departments are grouped

around the terrace. The circulation between the two towers is connected through and around the public pieces at the terrace level. There is also an education center, which will be in the later phase. It will have classrooms and a café. A small amphitheater will be an outdoor classroom. We thought that the smoking professors would like that, because they could smoke and teach at the same time. But the

furniture, nice light, and a better relationship to your staff and your colleagues—if you think I'm here to do that, you're crazy. I wouldn't do that to you." Finally, she laughed.

Anyway, I'm not making fun of them, because that's human nature, and I would do a lot of the same thing. I told them that. I said, "When it comes to buying clothes I go to Brooks Brothers because I don't want to deal with it. So I understand that assumption. But it's not about fashion. It's about breaking out of your security blanket."

I sent them down to the Rouse Company [a 1974 Gehry project in Columbia, Maryland] before they hired us. I said, "This is a long shot for me. I haven't been there in years. I don't know what it's like now; I don't know if they like it or if they're using it, or if they've kept it intact." But I said, "That's the last time I did a project like this. In that project, we were very inventive; we invented lighting and all kinds of things that hadn't been done in that arena at that point. So my suggestion to you is, rather than interview me, go down there and talk to them, and ask them how it is. If I do the building, I'm going to start there, and I'm going to try to create an environment for the future." They went, and they came back ecstatic. They loved it! They talked to all the people, and the people told them how it works, and they're very proud of it, and it's flexible, and it does all the things we planned for it.

design process models showing the building's development

amphitheater is another way of transitioning from grade up onto the plaza.

We haven't selected materials yet, but the thinking is that on the north side of the building, because the light is more diffuse, we can let in more of it without disturbing the computers. Computer glare is a big issue on this project, because all the labs are filled with screens. So we're thinking we can open up the north side with a curtain wall, and close up the south with punch windows so we can control the light. We're thinking in terms of light tracks, skylights that are skinny cuts in the building that will bring light down through the middle. They don't really want huge atrium spaces. They're engineers, so everything has to be useful. The cracks are a way of bringing in light without wasting a lot of space.

The warehouse has the same program as the towers, a mixture of office and lab space. But it has a higher floor-to-floor ratio, because the labs have special height requirements. For example, there is a lab called the Leg Lab, where they build artificial limbs that are self-locomoting robots. They worked on the one that went to Mars. They store all the old robots—they hang them up. Rob Brooks, who runs the robot program proposed making the building emotional. He thought of the whole building as an experiment, as a robot, and so he suggested that maybe the building should blush or cry or, you know, express what's going on within it somehow. He also wants to build robot window washers for us in case we have areas of the building that a person can't get to.

We made interior models in the preschematic phase. We showed them in order to get a reaction. They are very loosely based on the program, and they are kind of experimental. We learned a lot by doing it, because some of them got better reactions than others. We brought them all and showed them to the client committee, which consisted of professors from several disciplines. The schemes are all based on

281

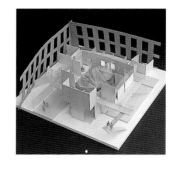

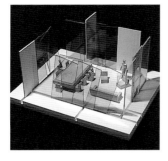

The 324,000-square-foot Stata Complex will house the Laboratory for Computer Science, the Artificial Intelligence Laboratory, the Laboratory for Information and Decision Systems, and the Linguistics and Philosophy Department. In addition, the program for the Stata Complex includes an auditorium and four major classrooms that will serve the Electrical Engineering and Computer Science departments, as well as common areas for the research community. Currently, the Stata Complex also includes a service facility, new locker rooms, assignable space, and a childcare facility.

The Stata Complex is the first phase of a new Master Plan designed by Frank O. Gehry & Associates that addresses the future development of the Northeast Sector of the main MIT campus. Future phases anticipate the creation of a Teaching and Learning Center, and the expansion of Building 68 that houses the Biology Department. The basic articulation of the major program sectors is driven by two fundamental requirements that are not easily reconciled. The goal of the Stata Complex is to be connected to the rest of the MIT campus, but the most fundamental components of the project must also be separated from the campus, specifically from the Infinite Corridor (the underground corridor that connects all of the campus buildings). Therefore, two distinct circulation patterns will be developed and organized in parallel, one public (for undergraduate students) and one private (for researchers).

The design of the research spaces is being developed around the

different cultures, different human or animal cultures. We started with a Japanese house that had sliding screens. We told them that we were talking about flexibility, and in the Japanese traditional house you can open up all the doors and have a big public room, or you can divide them up so that no one knows what anyone else is doing. They hated it. It was too much decision making, too many choices,

too much neatness required on everyone's part. They didn't identify with that at all. The scheme that did get a positive reaction was the orangutan village. They would live in little nests in the trees. Each person would have one. And then they would come down onto the Savannah in the daytime, and work collectively. That made a lot of sense to them. There's a division in their lives between the private inward rou-

tine and the collective lab work that they do in big groups.

People don't understand the importance of the involvement of the client, which is huge. That was not true of beaux arts architecture at all, but it is very true of Frank's architecture. It's important for people to understand that these things don't happen by magic; they happen because the client wants them to; it's not an accident.

office study models

opposite:
design process model

concept of neighborhoods. In the Stata Complex, these neighborhoods will expand vertically as well as horizontally and thus they become architectural spaces. The typical floor layout will be based on flexibility principals, with modular office wings that are L-shaped and U-shaped located around flexible laboratory space. The central neighborhood lounge will mediate the various independent spaces and will become the connector between the neighborhoods. From the lounge, one will be able to overlook one's own neighborhood and to look up to the neighborhoods above.

The massing of the Stata Complex involves two towers sitting on a wide base. These three elements meet on the roof of the base between the towers, which is the heart of the Stata Complex. It will feature public and private terraces and gardens. The towers are articulated as wings, and they open to the heart of the complex and cradle it. This winglike articulation of the towers allows the differentiation of the lab and department identities without creating actual barriers between them.

client: Massachusetts Institute of Technology

project principals: Frank O. Gehry, design principal
Jim Glymph, project principal
Craig Webb, project designer
Marc Salette, project architect

project team: Rachel Allen, Anna Helena Berge, Christopher Barbee, Herwig Baumgartner, Tomaso Bradshaw, Dari Iron, Michael Kempf, Andrew Matt, Clifford Minnick, Robyn Morgenstern, David Plotkin, Robert Seelenbacher, Dennis Sheldon, Derek Sola, Steven Traeger, Brian Zamora

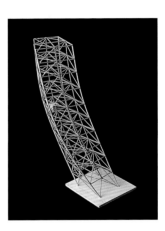

modena gate 1998–
Modena, Italy

This project is for an arts festival that's to go on for two years. It's similar to the Spoleto Festival. It started in June 1998. They want to have the gate next winter, and it will stay up until the end of the festival. I went to Modena because my friend Irving Lavin [Princeton art historian] asked me about it. He was on a committee for the festival, and he asked me if I could stop in Modena on my way somewhere. He was there, and he wanted to introduce me to the mayor.

I went to the meeting, and the mayor showed us the sites and told us the history of the idea. I said, "Well, what's the budget for this project?" and the mayor said, "A million dollars." I said, "Well, you can't do very much for that, but I'd be willing to try to do something, but it would probably have to be a temporary kind of thing." The mayor said, "No, no, it has to be something permanent; we can't afford to spend a million dollars on something temporary." I said, "Well, how adventurous are you?" And he said, "Try me."

So we shook right there. Then I said, "Okay, here's the idea. I'm going to get two or three construction cranes, and I'm going to create a…." He looked at me and he looked at Irving, and Irving started laughing and said, "Well, I told you, Mister Mayor, that the least expected…." He said, "I'm shocked, too." I said, "Well, if you don't like it, I don't even know if we can do it, but we'll pursue it. I'll do all the research. If I can do it, I'll do it; if not, I'll let you know." So we did some research, and found that we could do it, and we're proceeding.

Then I called Massimo Colomban, our friend in Treviso, and said, "Massimo, we have a problem for you." He said, "Naturally we'll do it. What is the problem?" I told him "I need some cranes," and he said, "Okay." Then he found us three cranes for free. So now we have to put the scrims on, and make them move slowly. They form the gateway. The third, the little crane, uses a projector. I'm not going to do it like a rock concert. I'm going to do it quietly.

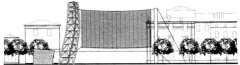

elevation looking east (screen in open and closed position)

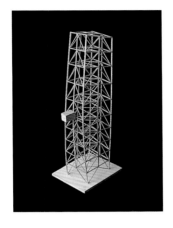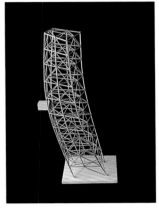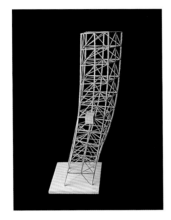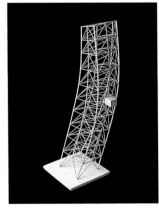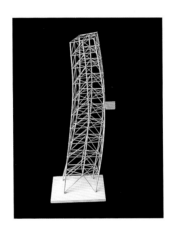

tomaso bradshaw: The project is a city gate. It is a temporary sculptural element at the end of the main piazza in Modena, to commemorate the arrival of the Duke d'Este four hundred years ago. The provincial capital moved to Modena and it became a powerful city-state, and Este's influence on the region was notable. There actually had been a gate there that was torn down in the early part of this century. Frank's idea is basically to put back the element that had closed off the whole piazza.

The project is on the periphery of the old city, on the Via Emilia, one of the most important roads in Italy. It is the primary entrance to Modena from the west. The city is famous now as Ferraris are manufactured near there, and it has a heavy industrial component.

There will be two layers of stainless-steel mesh. One might be colored, but essentially it's a series of layers that unfold, pull back up, and represent some kind of movement, similar to the Times Square project. The idea is to try to create a kinetic element. The gate will open and turn and move. The final layer is a scrim that is revealed as the gate opens. The tower rotates, the arm moves up and down, and the fabric itself becomes furled in, like a sail on a mast. With this method, if we choreograph the various layers correctly, we can get a kind of dance going in which, as one element is revealed, the other is concealed. It will be computer guided—probably a pretty simple system of gantries and winches that move along the arm and pull the mesh in, like a proscenium curtain on a stage.

Later: We tried with the cranes, and that's not going to work. So now the idea is to make a drawing in space with metal. It will be a gateway. We'll make a metal screen that will open and close, and that will be it. It will be a very baroque gate.

285

**views of two final
design models**

**opposite:
site model of initial
crane scheme**

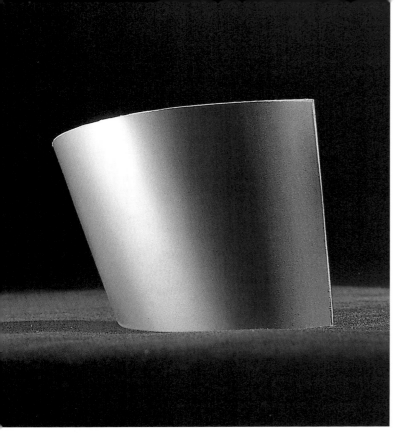

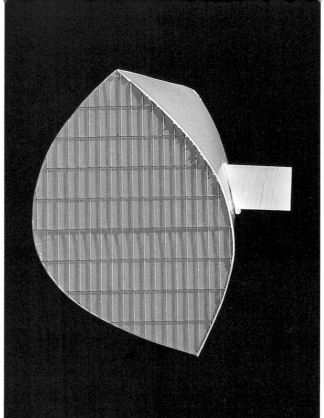

286

modena gate

We're getting a lot of little jobs like Modena. In Biloxi, Mississippi, we're going to do a study for a museum devoted to the ceramics of the amazing George Ohr. He was from Biloxi, and the mayor called me from there. He's putting up the money. They already have an architect, and now they're bringing a big gorilla in to style it for him! So I told the mayor, "I'm not going to come in and poach on some poor kid. It's not fair." But he insists that we're not to worry.

And then we have Maggie's two little hospices, one in Dundee and one in Cambridge. Maggie Cheswick-Jencks, who died of cancer a couple of years ago, started a little hospice program called Maggie's Place. They built one in Edinburgh, and it's really sweet. She supervised it. Now that she's gone, they've asked me to do one in Cambridge, England. I said yes. I haven't started working on it. It's tiny. The budget is half-a-million dollars. I have to do it. Probably for free. Maggie left money for it. That can be my sculpture. The people who are running it said, "The one in Cambridge isn't a very good site, and we've found another site in Dundee that's better." I said, "Well, what are you going to do with poor Cambridge?" "Oh, we'll get some other..." I said, "Oh, come on, I'll do them both. As long as I'm doing one, I'll do two."

client: City of Modena   **project team:** Ana Henton   287

project principals: Frank O. Gehry, design principal
Jim Glymph, project principal
Craig Webb, project designer
Tomaso Bradshaw, project architect

final design model of site

**opposite:
design process model of
information kiosk**

venice **gateway** 1998–
Venice, Italy

We're just starting a study for the harbor in Venice—a dream project. It is near the airport, where boats come to pick up passengers on their way to the city. It's the same size as the museum in Bilbao. It will include a huge terminal building and a conference center. They're currently rebuilding the airport.

It took a while to get them focused on a good program, because they started out with office buildings, and it didn't make sense. That's why we delayed working on it. We kept trying to work on it, and we couldn't work on it. We kept calling them and saying their program didn't make sense, it didn't fit, and we kept challenging them. And finally, they went back and figured out this program, which is incredible! This program

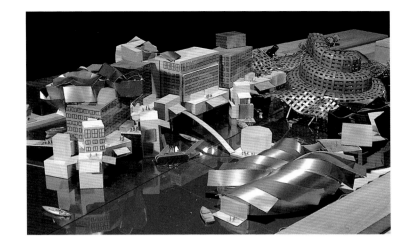

really makes sense, and will be used and will be successful if they build it.

The question: do we make an absolutely new thing that has nothing to do with Venice, or do we make a kind of homage to Venice but not like the real Venice, real architecture. I'm not going to do either of those things. I'll probably make a new thing, and since it's on the water, it will look like it relates to Venice. It will have a familial relationship. I want it to be a festive welcome to Venice. So the scale, the program, everything is pretty nice now. There are a few little things that have to be ironed out. The relationship to the airport itself is still unresolved. How do you get to the airport from the gateway? They want to build a moving sidewalk system. You'll have to take three moving sidewalks to get to the airport once you get off the boat. But then, for the rich people, they're going to have a taxi channel that goes right to the airport, and there's a lagoon there. So in other words, some people will never stop at this place, but go directly to the airport in the water taxi. But I'm trying to change that. If you're going to make this thing work, you have to have everything come there. They have to have *vaporettos* [steam ferries that provide public transport for pedestrians] because everybody can't afford a water taxi.

So far, we're only hired to do the study. Well, let's hope they stick with it. The airport director loves me. Loves this thing. He's an elected official. You know what happens to elected officials? They go out of office. So you've got to get work done quickly. Bilbao was six months from disaster. Six months later it wouldn't have happened because there was a change in the bureaucracy. Even the minister of culture was very skeptical about the building. She's an educator in elementary and high schools and she wasn't that interested in architecture and the arts. She's a complete convert now because it's successful.

We have a couple of things on our side in Venice. The mayor is a philosopher. He was a Tafuri follower, a rationalist, and he teaches at the university. That group is suspicious of people like me. Francesco Dal Co is on my side, and he will have a say. The architects in town can create problems, because they don't want people like me in there. For instance, we showed them the model when they were here. They loved it. But then they started to think of showing it back in Venice. It was very interesting the way they started backpedaling. They said, "It's too rough, it looks too flamboyant, we'll get a lot of criticism." I said, "Well, do you want me to do it or not?" "Oh yeah, we want a strong building." But my stuff in these sketchy models looks a little unfinished. We've got to show them the first models for Disney Hall, and how it evolved.

**design process model of
site plan and detail (opposite)**

site plan

edwin chan: After Bilbao, we are looking for a sequel, and a lot of what is out there I don't see as a sequel. Venice has the potential to be a sequel that is going to be better than the original. It's literally in the water. It will have a kind of ambiguity between an indoor space and an outdoor space, as it's also dry and wet, with the water and the boats.

What they want is a place of arrival. So it has conference centers and a place for people to rest and hang out. There will be a hotel near it. It's going to be a facility that supports the airport. So presumably, with the new airport now under construction, when finished the volume of traffic will pick up. In addition to being a terminal for water taxis, it will have other facilities that will enhance or support the transferring of passengers from the airport into Venice. There will be people who come here to wait for the next flight, for example, or they may have a conference or a convention to attend. There is going to be food and there will be lounges. The challenge is about moving volumes of people through and creating places where they can rest. Hopefully, the project will help organize all of those things. We're going to have a big room (we know that already) that is going to float on top of the water. I imagine it will be like a piazza, an urban space that is floating on the sea.

Conceptual Design Phase: The "Venice Gateway," situated at the Marco Polo airport on the mainland, is part of a large-scale redevelopment of the airport, including the construction of a new terminal, infrastructure, and parking facilities. As a separate component of this development, Frank O. Gehry & Associates has been commissioned to develop a proposal for a business hotel and conference center.

The site occupies the basin adjacent to the existing airport terminal, at the head of the canal that leads to the lagoon and the city. This basin, which accommodates the airport water-taxi and bus-boat facilities, will be significantly enlarged following completion of the new terminal. The new terminal will be linked to the site via a canal, and all water traffic to Venice will pass through this basin. In addition, the old terminal, service facilities and parking structures adja-

cent to the site will continue to operate, creating significant traffic and movement in the vicinity. The conceptual site design takes advantage of this location by placing the bulk of the program directly on the water. The program is divided into three primary components: a 300-room luxury hotel, a conference center, and an entertainment/commercial/retail/and transportation facilities area. The total program comprises approximately 30,000 m^2.

In addition to its siting on the water, the project also relates to Venice through the shape and color of the exterior surfaces. The guestrooms are housed in several separate components forming a tight, irregular arc of buildings. These elements stand on the lobby level plinth and are connected by bridges and stairs. The hotel lobby, guestrooms, and theater are clad in plaster; the rooftop restaurant

is finished in metal. The conference center, entertainment, and retail components are also proposed as metal structures. The metal buildings especially are designed with curved walls and roofs, enhancing the reflective properties of the skin. The colors of the metal and plaster components are based on Venetian sources. The variety of colors is intended to complement the architectural massing, breaking down the overall scale of the project, and enlivening the light reflected off the water.

detail of design process model

opposite:
night view of the model

client: Aeroporto di Venezia Marco Polo S.p.A.SAVE

project principals: Frank O. Gehry, design principal
Randy Jeffeerson, project principal
Edwin Chan, project designer
Tomaso Bradshaw, project architect

project team: Kamran Ardalan,
Ana Henton, Ross Miller,
David Nam, Dan Pohrte,
Beat Schenk

frank o. gehry

one-man
exhibitions   *Frank Gehry: Unique Fish Lamps,* Larry Gagosian Gallery, Los Angeles, California, 21 March–14 April 1984

Frank Gehry Recent Drawings, Ballenford Architectural Books, Toronto, Canada, 15 October–30 November 1984

Frank Gehry: Fish and Snake Lamps, Metro Pictures, New York, New York, November–December 1984

Frank O. Gehry: Recent Projects, Gallery MA, Tokyo, Japan, October–November 1985

Frank O. Gehry: Castello di Rivoli, Turin, Italy, March–May 1986

Frank O. Gehry: New Cardboard Furniture, Hoffman/Borman Gallery, Los Angeles, California, February–March 1988

The Architecture of Frank Gehry, this retrospective was organized by Walker Art Center, Minneapolis, Minnesota, 20 September–30 November 1986. The exhibition traveled to Contemporary Art Museum, Houston, Texas, Art Gallery at Harbourfront, Toronto, Canada, High Museum of Art, Atlanta, Georgia, Museum of Contemporary Art, Los Angeles, California, and Whitney Museum of American Art, New York, New York

The Work of Frank Gehry, Galerie für Architektur und Raum, Berlin, West Germany, 1989

Frank O. Gehry, Architekturmuseum in Basel, Switzerland, September 1989

Frank O. Gehry: Sketches of Recent Projects, The Art Store Gallery, Los Angeles, California, October–November, 1989

Frank O. Gehry, Center of Contemporary Art, Warsaw, Poland, May–June 1990

Frank O. Gehry, deSingel Museum, Antwerp, Belgium, September–November 1990

Frank O. Gehry: The Architect's Sketchbook and Contemporary Design, The Getty Center, Santa Monica, California, September 1990–January 1991

Frank O. Gehry, Centraal Museum, Utrecht, The Netherlands, November 1990

Frank O. Gehry, Arkitektur Museet, Stockholm, Sweden, November 1990–January 1991

Frank O. Gehry (furniture and lamps), b.d. Madrid Gallery, Madrid, Spain, December 1990. The exhibition traveled to Barcelona at the Madrid Gallery, January 1991

Frank O. Gehry, Projets en Europe, Centre Georges Pompidou, Paris, France, March–June 1991

Frank O. Gehry, Dansk Arkitekturcenter, Kobenhavn, Denmark, March 1991

Frank O. Gehry, Can Reekum Museum, Apeldoorn, The Netherlands, June–September 1991

Frank Gehry: New Bentwood Furniture Designs, Musée des Arts Décoratifs de Montréal, Montréal, Canada, 1992

Frank O. Gehry: New Bentwood Furniture Designs, St. Louis Art Museum, St. Louis, Missouri, 15 December 1992–14 February 1993

Frank O. Gehry, Vitra Design Museum, Weil am Rhein, Germany, 1994

Frank O. Gehry, University of Virginia, 7 April–15 May 1994. Exhibition in conjunction with the Thomas Jefferson Medal of Architecture.

Frank Gehry: European Projects, Aedes Gallerie und Arkitecturforum, Berlin, Germany, September–October 1994

Frank Gehry: Innovation in Furniture Design 1969 to the Present, The Wetsman Gallery of 20th Century Decorative Art, Birmingham, Michigan, 9 September–15 October 1994

Frank Gehry: A Study, Gagosian Gallery, Los Angeles, California, 18 March–1 May 1999

selected
exhibition designs   For the Los Angeles County Museum of Art, Los Angeles, California:

Art Treasures of Japan, 1965

Assyrian Reliefs, 1966

Billy Al Bengston Retrospective, 1968

Treasures of Tutankhamen, 1978

Avant-Garde of Russia, 1910–1930, 1980

Seventeen Artists in the Sixties, 1981

German Expressionist Sculpture, 1983

Degenerate Art, 1994

Exiles & Emigrés, 1997

Art of the Motorcycle, The Solomon R. Guggenheim Museum, New York, New York, 1998

opposite:
early design process model
of the atrium,
Guggenheim Museum Bilbao

awards, fellowships, and
honorary degrees

Fellow, American Institute of Architects, 1974
Arnold W. Brunner Memorial Prize in Architecture, American Academy of Arts and Letters, 1977
Fellow, American Academy of Arts and Letters, 1987
Honorary Doctorate of Visual Arts, California Institute of the Arts, 1987
Honorary Doctorate of Fine Arts, Rhode Island School of Design, 1987
Pritzker Architecture Prize, Hyatt Foundation, 1989
Trustee, American Academy in Rome, 1989
Honorary Doctorate of Engineering, Technical University of Nova Scotia, 1989
Honorary Doctorate of Fine Arts, Otis Art Institute, 1989
Fellow, American Academy of Arts and Sciences, 1991
Wolf Prize in Art, Wolf Foundation, 1992
Praemium Imperiale Award, Japan Art Association, 1992
Honorary Doctorate of Humanities, Occidental College, 1993
Dorothy and Lillian Gish Prize, Dorothy and Lillian Gish Prize Trust, 1994
Academician, National Academy of Design, 1994
Honorary Consul, Bilbao, Spain, 1997
Honorary Doctorate of Architecture, Southern California Institute of Architecture, 1997
Friedrich Kiesler Prize, Friedrich Kiesler Foundation, 1998
Honorary Academician, Royal Academy of Arts, 1998
Gold Medal, Royal Architectural Institute of Canada, 1998
Chancellor of the City of Bilbao, Spain, 1998
National Medal of the Arts, National Endowment for the Arts, 1998
Honorary Doctor of Law, University of Toronto, 1998
AIA Gold Medal, American Institute of Architects, 1999

In addition, Mr. Gehry has received over one hundred awards from the American Institute of Architects to honor outstanding architectural design.

major
publications

Arnell, Peter and Ted Bickford, *Frank Gehry, Buildings and Projects* (New York: Rizzoli International Publications, 1985).
Friedman, Mildred (ed.), *The Architecture of Frank Gehry* (New York: Rizzoli International Publications, 1986).
Marquez, Cecilia F.(ed.), "Frank O. Gehry," *El Croquis 45*,
   El Croquis Editorial, Madrid, October/November 1990.
Frank Gehry: New Bentwood Furniture Designs, The Montreal Museum of Decorative Arts, 1992
Futugawa, Yukio, "Frank O. Gehry," *GA Architect 10*, EDITA Tokyo Company, Ltd., Tokyo, 1993.
Marquez, Cecilia F. (ed.), "Frank O. Gehry: 1991–1995,"
   El Croquis 74/75, El Croquis Editorial, Madrid, December 1995.
Van Bruggen, Coosje, *Frank O. Gehry: Guggenheim Museum Bilbao*
   (New York: The Solomon R. Guggenheim Foundation, 1997).
Dal Co, Francesco and Kurt W. Forster, *Frank O. Gehry, The Complete Works* (New York: The Monacelli Press, 1998).
Bechtler, Cristina (ed.), *Art and Architecture in Discussion:*
   Frank O. Gehry/Kurt W. Forster (Cantz Verlag, 1999).

**opposite:
DG Bank at Pariser Platz,
design process model of
"The Horse's Head"**

acknowledgments   This is the second time I have had the opportunity to work on a book with Frank Gehry. The first was the catalogue for his Walker Art Center exhibition in 1986. The current adventure was inspired by his "new office," which since 1986 has grown exponentially in size, technology, and expertise. The most significant change has been the addition of his two partners, Jim Glymph and Randy Jefferson, who have made Gehry's wildest architectural dreams come true. I thank them for talking with me about the new office methodology. Many staff members have been extremely generous with their time and knowledge, including Edwin Chan, Craig Webb, Rachel Allen, and Tomaso Bradshaw.

This book could not have happened without the wisdom and efforts of Keith Mendenhall, who is responsible for the Gehry archive—photographic and written—and who has provided all of the essential documentation for the projects in this volume. Equally crucial in this endeavor has been Tracey Shiffman, who has designed this book with great skill and collaborated with Frank's office in organizing and selecting all of its visual material; she deserves endless admiration and thanks. My thanks and respect as well to Michael Sorkin for his witty, insightful essay. Chris Herrlinger, Frank Gehry's assistant, has arranged my trips to Los Angeles, and helped make the schedule work. Keith Mendenhall has been ably assisted by Laura Stella. We are indebted to the many photographers who have provided images for this book; particular recognition is due Leslie Brenner, Josh White, and Whit Preston. David Morton and Solveig Williams of Rizzoli Publications have lent support from the start, and I thank them for their patience and encouragement.

To Frank and Berta Gehry, whose warm hospitality and friendship have made my trips to Los Angeles both stimulating and fruitful, I am ever indebted.

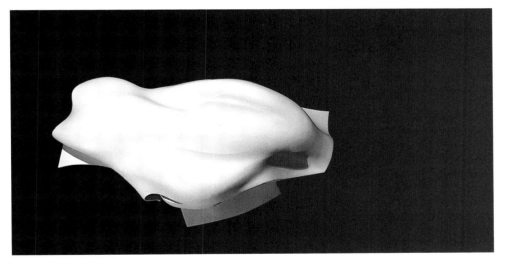

Mildred Friedman

Boldface page references are
used to designate illustrations;
italic boldface references are
used for principal discussions.

297